Expert Advice From The Home Depot®

Kitche
Design and Planning
1-2-3®

Meredıth®
BOOKS

Home Depot® Books
An imprint of Meredith® Books

Kitchen Design and Planning 1-2-3®
Senior Editor: John P. Holms
Art Director: Tom Wegner
Writers: Catherine Hamrick, Meg Goodman Richards
Contributing Writers: Linda Eggerss, Mary Thompson Jones
    Katie L. Smith, Shelley Stewart
Copy Chief: Terri Fredrickson
Copy and Production Editor: Victoria Forlini
Editorial Operations Manager: Karen Schirm
Managers, Book Production: Pam Kvitne,
Marjorie J. Schenkelberg, Rick von Holdt
Manufacturing and Inventory Control Manger: Mark Weaver
Contributing Copy Editor: Sharon McHaney, Margaret Smith
Contributing Proofreaders: Janet Anderson, Julie Cahalan,
    David Craft, Kathi DiNicola, Sara Henderson, Terri Krueger
Illustrator: Jim Swanson
Indexer: Donald Glassman
Electronic Production Coordinator: Mary Lee Gavin
Editorial and Design Assistants: Renee E. McAtee,
    Karen McFadden

Editorial and Design Contributions:
Abramowitz, Staub & Associates, Inc.
Designer: Tim Abramowitz
Editor: Catherine M. Staub

Meredith® Books
Editor in Chief: Linda Raglan Cunningham
Design Director: Matt Strelecki
Executive Editor, Gardening and Home Improvement:
    Benjamin W. Allen

Publisher: James D. Blume
Executive Director, Marketing: Jeffrey Myers
Executive Director, New Business Development: Todd M. Davis
Director, Sales-Home Depot: Robb Morris
Executive Director, Sales: Ken Zagor
Director, Operations: George A. Susral
Director, Production: Douglas M. Johnston
Business Director: Jim Leonard

Vice President and General Manager: Douglas J. Guendel

Meredith Publishing Group
President, Publishing Group: Stephen M. Lacy
Vice President-Publishing Director: Bob Mate

Meredith Corporation
Chairman and Chief Executive Officer: William T. Kerr

In Memoriam: E. T. Meredith III (1933-2003)

Photographers
Image Studios
Account Executive: Lisa Egan
Primary Photography: Bill Rein, Glen Hartjes, Dave Wallace
Contributing Photography: Dave Classon, Bill Kapinski, Shane Van
Boxtel, John von Dorn,
Remodeling Consultant: Rick Nadke
Assistants: Mike Clines, Roger Wilmers
Stylists: BJ Hill, Karla Kaphaem, Dawn Koehler

The Home Depot®
Licensing Specialist: Ilana Wilensky

Note to the Reader: Due to differing conditions, tools, and
individual skills, Meredith Corporation and The Home Depot®
assume no responsibility for any damages, injuries suffered, or
losses incurred as a result of following the information published
in this book. Before beginning any project, review the
instructions carefully, and if any doubts or questions remain,
consult local experts or authorities. Because codes and
regulations vary greatly, you always should check with
authorities to ensure that your project complies with all
applicable local codes and regulations. Always read and observe
all of the safety precautions provided by any tool
or equipment manufacturer, and follow all accepted safety
procedures.

The editors of *Kitchen Design and Planning 1-2-3®* are dedicated
to providing accurate and helpful do-it-yourself information. We
welcome your comments about improving this book and ideas
for other books we might offer to home improvement
enthusiasts.

If you would like to purchase any of our home improvement,
cooking, crafts, gardening, or home decorating and design books,
check wherever quality books are sold. Or visit us at:
meredithbooks.com

Contact us by any of these methods:
Leave a voice message at: 800/678-2093
Write to: Meredith Books, Home Depot Books
        1716 Locust St.
        Des Moines, IA 50309–3023
Send e-mail to: hi123@mdp.com

Take our quick survey and enter to win a $1,000 gift card from The Home Depot®

Thank you for choosing this book! To serve you better, we'd like to know a little more about your interests. Please take a minute to fill out this survey and drop it in the mail. As an extra-special "thank-you" for your help, we'll enter your name into a drawing to win a $1,000 Home Depot Gift Card!

WIN THIS CARD!
OFFICIAL SWEEPSTAKES RULES AND ENTRY DETAILS ON BACK.
No purchase necessary to enter or win.

PLEASE MARK ONE CIRCLE PER LINE IN EACH OF THE NUMBERED COLUMNS BELOW WITH DARK PEN OR PENCIL:

1 My interest in the areas below is:

Cooking	High Interest	Average Interest	No Interest
Gourmet & Fine Foods	◯	◯	◯
Quick & Easy	◯	◯	◯
Healthy/Natural	◯	◯	◯

Decorating	High Interest	Average Interest	No Interest
Country	◯	◯	◯
Traditional	◯	◯	◯
Contemporary	◯	◯	◯

Do-It-Yourself	High Interest	Average Interest	No Interest
Home Repair	◯	◯	◯
Remodeling	◯	◯	◯
Home Decor	◯	◯	◯

(painting, wallpapering, window treatments, etc.)

Gardening	High Interest	Average Interest	No Interest
Flowers	◯	◯	◯
Vegetables	◯	◯	◯
Landscaping	◯	◯	◯

2 My plans to do a project in the following areas within the next 6 months are:

	High Interest	Average Interest	No Interest
Bathroom Remodel	◯	◯	◯
Kitchen Remodel	◯	◯	◯
Storage Project	◯	◯	◯
Plumbing	◯	◯	◯
Wiring	◯	◯	◯
Interior Painting	◯	◯	◯
Window Treatments	◯	◯	◯
Plant/Plan a Flower Garden	◯	◯	◯
Plant/Plan a Vegetable Garden	◯	◯	◯
Deck Building	◯	◯	◯
Patio Building	◯	◯	◯
Landscape Improvements	◯	◯	◯

3 I estimate that I have spent this amount of money on home improvement projects in the past 6 months:
Less than $1,000 ◯ $1,000-$2,500 ◯ $2,500-$5,000 ◯ $5,000-$10,000 ◯ $10,000 or more ◯

4 I purchased this book ◯   This book was a gift ◯

5 You *must* fill out all of the requested information below to enter to win a $1,000 Home Depot Gift Card.

Name:

Address: Apt. or Suite #

Daytime telephone number: (   )

City:

State/Province: Country: Zip:

For D-I-Y trend research, please tell us your gender: Male ◯   Female ◯

Also, E-mail me with information of interest to me.

E-mail address:

Thank you for completing our survey! Please mail today to have your name entered to win a $1,000 Home Depot Gift Card. But hurry—one winner will be selected soon. See rules on back for entry deadline. To find more home improvement tips, visit www.homedepot.com or www.meredithbooks.com.

KDP204

A. LETTERFOLD TOWARD BOTTOM OF SURVEY FORM, ALONG ORANGE TRIANGLES AT LEFT AND RIGHT.

B. MOISTEN BOTTOM STRIP, LETTERFOLD TOWARD TOP OF FORM, ALONG ORANGE TRIANGLES AT LEFT AND RIGHT.

Canadian customers:
See mailing details on back!

▲ FOLD CAREFULLY ALONG ORANGE DASHED LINES ABOVE ▲

Take our quick survey and enter to win a $1,000 gift card from The Home Depot®

No postage necessary if mailed *inside* the United States.
If mailed *outside* of the United States, letterfold survey form, place in an envelope, stamp, and mail to:

Meredith Corporation
Home Depot 1-2-3 Books (LN-104)
1716 Locust Street
Des Moines, Iowa 50309-3023

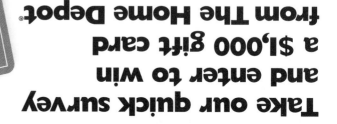

Expert Advice From The Home Depot®

Kitchen
Design and Planning
1-2-3®

Meredith® BOOKS

Kitchen Design and Planning 1-2-3®

Table of Contents

How To Use This Book

Improving your kitchen is an investment in the equity of your home, your quality of life, and a reflection of your style and taste. Putting in a new kitchen can be one of the largest single expenses you will make, so whether you intend to do all or part of the work yourself or plan to use the services of an architect or designer and bring in a contractor to manage the entire job, you'll need some know-how and some good advice.

That's why the designers and associates at The Home Depot have put everything they know about designing and planning a new kitchen in one easy-to-use book. *Kitchen Design and Planning 1-2-3* will guide you step-by-step through the often complex and bewildering process of replacing, upgrading, or remodeling the space that has become the center of the modern home.

Take It Step-by-Step— ■ Design ■ Plan ■ Install

Kitchen installation involves three distinct phases— creating a design, making a plan, and installing the components. How much time and effort is put into each phase will ultimately define how happy you'll be in your new kitchen. There aren't any shortcuts here. Every step is important.

A kitchen design that works is more than a floor plan and a lumber order; it's a package of information that will turn a dream into reality. A good design concept is a combination of style and function. It's the result of asking yourself the right questions; you define not only your personal style and taste, but also how you and your family want to use the space now and in the future. A good design focuses on the details. To get exactly what you want, you have to consider every element that will be part of your new kitchen, including appliances, cabinets, countertops, fixtures, floors, color, texture, lighting, surfaces, and window treatments.

A lot to think about? Absolutely. That's why you make a plan.

Make a Plan

The design concept will evolve into the plan for executing the installation. The plan will show you where the stove and sink go, the color of the trim on the cabinets, and the specifications for the light above the counter. It will ensure that you've complied with all the necessary building codes for safety before you begin tearing out the walls, and prepare you for visits from the building inspector along the way. The plan will also reflect spatial and dimensional guidelines established by the NKBA (National Kitchen and Bath Association) for ease of use. And the plan—in the form of working drawings, layouts, and elevations— will become the ultimate authority for contractors, carpenters, plumbers, electricians, or anyone else you might have working on your project—including yourself. Finally, a solid and accurate plan allows you to create a realistic schedule for the work, including lead time for ordering materials and timing their installation. A plan will help you focus on the big picture when the old countertops and cabinets are piled in the garage, the house is draped in sheets of plastic, and the plumbing is only half finished.

When you've completed the plan, you're ready to install the components.

Put It All Together

The first thing to remember is that no matter how well you've planned and how carefully you've scheduled, things are going to go wrong. You'll need a plan for solving problems as they come up. Some events will simply be out of your or your contractor's control—a shipping strike delays delivery on the cabinets or the granite countertop cracks while being unloaded. Other things, such as taking accurate measurements, complying with local codes, setting the right order of work, or securing well-defined contracts and work agreements are definitely in your control. The bottom line: Control what you can so you can deal as effectively as possible with the issues you can't.

Find What You Need

The seven chapters of *Kitchen Design and Planning 1-2-3* are organized to provide you with a logical and easy-to-follow guide.

■ Important concepts are cross-referenced throughout the book.

■ Charts and checklists can be photocopied, filled out, and filed to answer questions, solve problems, keep track of details, and evolve successful concepts.

■ Full-color photography and easy-to-understand illustrations clarify information at every stage of the process.

■ The combination of good design basics and practical advice make this book a hard-working and concise reference on every aspect of designing and planning a kitchen.

In short, working your way through *Kitchen Design and Planning 1-2-3* is like sitting across the table from a designer who's making sure you've thought of everything.

Look Inside

Chapter One: Style and Function
Understanding the basics of design and how to turn theory into practice.

Chapter Two: Inspiring Designs
Applying design theory to 10 basic kitchen shapes and styles.

Chapter Three: Planning
Defining your needs in order to draft layouts and floor plans and make decisions about what's going in the kitchen.

Chapter Four: Shopping Guide
Making informed buying decisions about cabinets, countertops, appliances, fixtures, lighting, flooring, and more.

Chapter Five: Fine Details
Finding finishing touches that make your kitchen your own.

Chapter Six: Universal Design
Planning for ease of living and access—now and in the future.

Chapter Seven: Remodeling Diary
Following the process of an actual installation from the first design conferences to tightening the last cabinet knob.

working with THE PROS

If you're not doing the job all by yourself, you may have already thought about hiring a contractor, a carpenter, an electrician, or a plumber. Give some thought also to working with someone who knows the whole process—a designer. Kitchen designers at The Home Depot—the people who helped write this book—work with the details of designing kitchens every day. If you've got questions, they've got answers. They'll be the first to tell you that renovating a kitchen is a big job, but the results are well worth it.

In fact, most home centers have highly qualified designers on staff, and their services are usually free. When there's a charge, it's part of the package if the home center does the job. Other retailers—including cabinet shops—usually have a designer on staff who will work much the same way. You can also consult outside interior designers and architects. You wouldn't be shy about hiring an electrician. Don't be shy about working with a designer either.

CHAPTER 1

Style and Function

A stylish and functional kitchen follows guidelines for traffic patterns, activity centers, storage, counter space, and system requirements.

Designing a successful kitchen means making the right decisions about everything from cabinetry and appliances, plumbing and electrical fixtures, to wall treatments and the style of flooring. The process involves planning, organization, scheduling, and dealing with the unexpected. The first step is creating a design that considers both style and function. The process is both creative and analytical and one in which you'll meet challenges and create solutions step-by-step.

CHAPTER 1 CONTENTS

left Quartz surfacing, a composite of natural stone, provides a countertop that is both beautiful and functional. The material is easy to clean and resists staining while offering a warm and elegant look. Style and function are always linked in good kitchen design.

Style

Many people think of style as it refers to popular themes in decorating such as country, Tuscan, Asian, traditional, French provincial, or contemporary. Style, when referred to in design, also defines a group of concepts (sometimes called principles) that help you make decisions about the look and feel of a room. The goal of the process is to create a kitchen that will accurately reflect your personal style and taste.

On the following pages you will learn about the basics of style and design—including color, texture, shape, line, form, pattern, detail, scale, proportion, unity, variety, balance, rhythm, and emphasis—and how each principle will affect the final design of your kitchen. In the second section of this chapter, you'll explore how to make your ideas functional. In the chapters that follow, you'll take what you've learned about style and function and apply them to planning the kitchen of your dreams.

above Exploring color options plays an important part of defining style. This is especially true when selecting cabinets which, aside from appliances, are the most visible part of your kitchen. Cabinet manufacturers offer many options, including natural woods and textured and painted finishes.

Understanding Color

Working with color is one of the most pleasurable aspects of decorating. A powerful element in design, color sets a room's tone and affects mood and emotion.

Warm colors, such as red and orange, convey cheer and liveliness, like a crackling fire. Yellow, a happy color, evokes a sunny day or daffodils bobbing in early spring. In northern climates or in rooms facing north, homeowners often incorporate warm colors as a counterpoint to cool temperatures and indirect sun. In contrast, cool colors communicate calm. The greens of leaves and grasses are restful. You may associate a blue sea with calm and

a faraway purple mountain with dignity. Cool-color rooms facing south or in a hot climate appear to diminish heat. That's why you often see blues and greens in beach houses.

Color also affects how you perceive a space. Warm colors seem closer than they really are, whereas cool colors recede. For example, a dark red ceiling appears to be lower than if it were painted pale blue. An oak bookcase stands out against (or seems to advance from) a pale green wall; however, against a dark tan wall, it blends in. Use warm colors to make a room cozy and soft; cool, light colors open up space.

The Color Wheel

Understanding color involves more than noticing its impact on your perception. The color wheel, which organizes the visible spectrum of colors and shows the relationships between them, is a useful tool in developing a color scheme.

There are 12 pure colors, those which have not been mixed with white or black, on the most commonly used color wheel.

Primary colors—red, yellow, and blue—are equidistant from each other on the color wheel. Of all colors, they are the brightest. They cannot be created from any other colors.

Secondary colors—orange, green, and violet—are derived from mixing equal parts of the primary colors. Red and yellow yields orange; yellow and blue, green; blue and red, violet.

Tertiary colors result from mixing an equal part of one primary and its adjacent secondary color: red-violet, red-orange, yellow-orange, yellow-green, blue-green, and blue-violet.

The 12 pure colors are rarely used in interior decorating except for emphasis. They are too strong, or intense. Black and white are not colors—at least technically. However, they are used to make shades and tints of colors. Tone is how light or dark a color is.

Adding white to pure color diminishes its intensity, producing tints, or lighter versions, of that color. The more white that is used, the lighter the tint will be. (To make pastels, start with white and tint it with other colors.)

Mixing a pure color with black also reduces intensity and produces shades, or darker versions of the color. Mixing black with white produces gray.

Hue refers to the undiluted color from which a tint or shade is derived. The primary, secondary, and tertiary pure colors of the color wheel are all hues, as are the infinite number of colors that result from mixing them together. A color may have a wide range of tints and shades, but they all share the same hue.

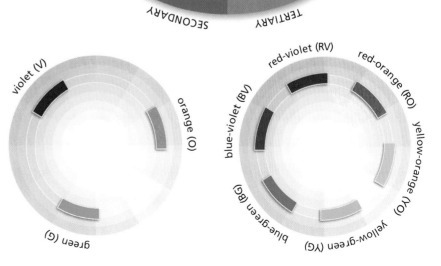

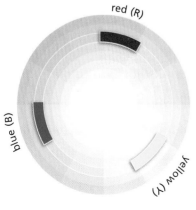

3 PRIMARY pure colors

3 SECONDARY pure colors

6 TERTIARY pure colors

Color and Light

Different types of lighting, as well as the amount, affect color. When making decisions about color, test swatches or paint chips in the actual space and under the lighting conditions in which the colors will be used.

Compared to sunlight, incandescent light makes objects appear redder and warmer; reducing the amount of light with a dimmer enhances the effect. Fluorescent light, typically cooler than sunlight, makes colors seem washed out. To counteract this cold effect, install lamps that approximate daylight or select warm colors for the room. Look for bulb types designated daylight or warm white.

When testing color samples, also bear in mind that color becomes stronger as it covers more area. For example, the red on a small paint chip becomes stronger on a wall.

The color wheel comes in handy when you're planning a color scheme for your kitchen. These basic schemes, which illustrate color harmony, will get you started.

Color Schemes

Monochromatic Colors

A monochromatic scheme uses the tints and shades of a single color. For example, look at a color card from a paint center; it shows paint chips in a range of tints and shades for one color. A single-color scheme will result in a serene or simple kitchen. Begin by selecting a single color; then add interest by mixing in that color's shades and tints. The darker and lighter hues keep the eye moving, preventing boredom. Some white color schemes use cooler whites to recede an area, or to contrast and intensify warm whites.

In a monochromatic scheme, three different tones generally work. The space needs deep-colored areas, mid-tones, and highlights. For instance, to create a successful all-white scheme, pick a yellow-tinted (versus a blue- or gray-tinted) white paint for the overall room color. The yellow tinting imparts a warm look, like a slightly aged patina. For the trim you might choose creamy white. For surfaces such as flooring and countertops avoid sterile white. Choose materials that are warm white.

The more contrast between the tones, the more energy a room exudes. The subtler the tones, the more quiet the mood.

above This slice of the color wheel shows all the tints of yellow-orange. Combining these tints and shades will create a monochromatic color scheme.

left A monochromatic scheme offers many options on the basic color through the use of tints and shades.

Analogous Colors

Analogous colors are neighbors on the color wheel. An analogous scheme is rich and soothing. If you start with blue as a foundation, you might pull in adjacent colors from the wheel, such as violet and green. For layered interest blend in tones of the intermediate colors of blue-violet and blue-green. The trick is to allow one color to dominate the combination. Study the color wheel to come up with other analogous color schemes, such as red-orange-yellow or orange-yellow-green.

above Textures and tints of yellow and yellow-green create a color palette of depth and contrast.

left This section of the color wheel shows all the tints and shades of yellow and yellow-green, creating an analogous color scheme.

Complementary Colors

A complementary scheme incorporates opposite colors—such as violet and yellow, red and green, or orange and blue—on the color wheel. These combinations energize a space. Rooms in which a lot of activity occurs, such as kitchens and dining rooms, are candidates for a complementary scheme. The trick to a complementary scheme is allowing one color to take center stage. Weave its counterpart color into the setting with fabric, trim, or accessories. Use complementary hues of the same intensity.

above A pleasing blend of complementary colors is evident in this red and green scheme.

left The color wheel shows all tints and shades of red and green that create a complementary color scheme.

above The strong colors in this scheme prove an agreeable and pleasing combination.

right These sections of the color wheel show all tints of orange, yellow-orange, and blue-violet that create an analogous color scheme with complementary accents.

Analogous Colors with Complementary Accents

Analogous colors with complementary accents make a pleasing color scheme. An example would include orange, yellow-orange, and the complementary color blue-violet. To lower the intensity of this combination, use tints and shades. Place complementary accents in several strategic locations or use it as a single focal point.

above A triadic scheme offers drama even when the tints and shades are subtle. Also try combining pure colors.

right These sections of the color wheel show all the tints and shades of yellow-orange, blue-green, and red-violet, creating a triadic color scheme.

Triadic Colors

A triadic color scheme uses three colors equidistant from one another on the color wheel. The primary colors of red, blue, and yellow are an example. Combining the secondary colors of orange, green, and violet is another. Achieving a successful triadic scheme of tertiary colors such as red-violet, yellow-orange, and blue-green is challenging. Such a combination usually requires moderation by using tints or shades instead of pure colors. You can control this vibrant scheme by limiting it to a small area and using it in concert with a neutral color, such as white.

left Wooden steps offer a clean transition up and into the kitchen from the tiled floor of the entryway. The pale green entryway walls frame the strongly grained patterns of the flooring and cabinetry. Cornice shelving makes a pleasing for display and the horizontal lines also move the eye cleanly into the kitchen space.

Line, Shape, and Form

A room has different **lines,** such as the edges of a countertop or where the floor and wall meet, each of which leaves an impression. The vertical lines of a column communicate stability. The horizontal lines of a floor or ceiling suggest rest. A diagonal line, such as a slanted ceiling, gives a sense of movement. The curved line of a countertop following the shape of an oval sink seems softer or less rigid than a right angle formed by a horizontal and vertical line. Lines create interest, contributing to the style of a room. However, overuse can distract. Too many diagonal lines, for instance, forces too much movement in a space.

The eye also is drawn to simple, complete geometric **shapes,** such as circles, squares, rectangles, or triangles. In contrast, an incomplete shape creates tension. You may see these shapes in the planes that make up walls, the floor, the ceiling, and countertops. Rectangular shapes often dominate a room. A room is most pleasing when the shapes are harmonious.

You also can discern shape based on where objects are placed. For instance, a large rectangular space that is an extension of an open-plan kitchen may be divided into two areas: one for dining and one for sitting.

Form is seen in furniture as well. For example, clean, minimal shapes characterize furniture dating from the modern period of the late 1920s to the early 1960s. Deep, cushy chairs used in casual seating do not have such crisp outlines. Whatever its form, furniture needs to be functional—meaning comfortable.

right The square countertop tiles of the built-in hutch contrast with the diamond pattern of the backsplash. The surface of the upper cabinets and the nickel pulls are smooth compared to the textured glass windows. The recessed panels of the lower cabinet doors are beaded board, introducing more texture and a rectangular pattern.

above Decorative crown moldings are good sources for variety in line and shape.

right In a monochromatic setting, texture plays a strong role because color is subdued.

Texture

The smoothness or roughness—actual or perceived—of a surface or object adds interest to the overall look of the room. In a monochromatic setting, variety takes a major role in the absence of different colors; woven or nubby fabrics for window treatments, wicker seating, a sisal mat or area rug under a breakfast table, or small accent pieces, such as baskets or carved candlesticks, add depth.

Texture is found in a variety of kitchen surfaces. Cabinets may be smooth laminate or rough-hewn hickory. A countertop may be granite or a smooth solid-surfacing. A floor may be ceramic tile or hardwood. A decorative finish on a wall, such as combing, gives visual texture while hiding any imperfections.

Match textures to the mood of the room. Heavily textured, nubby fabrics are suited to a casual eating area. Smooth, shiny surfaces are often equated with a contemporary look.

Texture also is linked with acoustics. Soft textures such as carpet absorb sound, whereas hard, smooth ones such as ceramic tile do not.

Pattern

Pattern occurs when a motif is repeated. Like texture, it adds interest. In a kitchen, different surfaces offer plenty of opportunities to use pattern. A backsplash might sport hand-painted decorative tiles or different colored tiles in a planned arrangement. Flooring patterns vary widely—same-size ceramic tiles, the repetition of a mix of large and small tiles, a rough brick floor, or a herringbone pattern in wood. You can select from many patterned wallcoverings or stencil a pattern on the walls.

Pattern can change how space is perceived. For example, vertical stripes make a surface appear taller and narrower, whereas horizontal stripes make it appear lower.

Pairing a single pattern with a solid color is always safe, but could seem dull. Mixing several patterns, however, can show decorating flair. Use patterns with a common texture, color, or motif. Vary the scale of patterns but not drastically; seat cushions with small checks are out of proportion with a large floral motif on a tablecloth.

right Panels in cabinet doors don't have to be limited to wooden insets or even glass. The woven panels in these cabinet doors are perfect examples of putting the principle of pattern to work.

below This monochromatic flooring pattern, which has the look of a rug, seems to point the way to the wooden floor of the kitchen straight ahead.

Detail

Details such as cabinet knobs and handles, trim and molding, or the right wall sconce or pendant light are the kinds of finishing touches that add depth and dimension to a kitchen. Hardware and lighting fixtures also lend a hand in defining style. Choose these important finishing touches as carefully as the more obvious parts of a kitchen, such as cabinetry, fixtures, flooring, or appliances. A door or window, for instance, draws more attention when framed by molding that is consistent with the overall design.

Details emphasize shape and line and help focus attention on major design elements.

Well-chosen details don't have to be small. Columns may mark the transition from a sitting area to an old-world or Tuscan-style kitchen with stucco walls. Details can be functional as well as decorative. A ceramic or stainless-steel backsplash protects walls from damage, but can also be an important design element. Carefully chosen details will distinguish a kitchen.

above The number of cabinet knobs and drawer pulls that are present in any kitchen make it easy to see why choosing the right ones is such an important design decision. These stylish pulls work well with simple raised-panel cabinet doors.

above right A colorful random pattern of ceramic tiles creates a backsplash to fill the space between wall cabinets and counters. Backsplashes can be made of a variety of materials including laminate, stone, or metal and offer the opportunity for custom finishing touches in a kitchen design.

right Decorative brackets add a level of traditional or old-world detail to an archway or entry that crown molding adds to a ceiling line. Brackets such as this one are accessories that can be purchased as part of a total cabinet package from many cabinet manufacturers.

Scale and Proportion

When you place elements in your kitchen that are appropriate to the size of the space and to one another, you will achieve proper **scale** and **proportion**. When scale and proportion are not applied, the design will have a disturbing effect. For instance, a giant dining room table in a tiny dining room will seem out of place. Your eyes and instincts are the best judges of appropriate scale and proportion.

right Connecting dining and kitchen spaces requires use of scale and proportion. The farm-style table and Country French chairs fill the space nicely without becoming overwhelming and the tile flooring with a detailed border both defines the dining area and helps separate it from the kitchen.

Unity and Variety

As an element of design, **unity** means harmony— experiencing parts of design as a whole rather than individually. For example, similar patterns or related colors of materials—including fabric, wallcoverings, rugs, and art—create unity.

Variety—expressed in different shapes, textures, or colors—keeps unity from becoming monotonous. For instance, to display white pottery, alternate different shapes so the collection carries visual weight.

Architectural unity is a powerful design element. The same molding may frame windows and doors that repeat similar vertical and horizontal lines. Inserting a corner wall might prevent monotony and add architectural interest. Upper and lower cabinets are often broken by a window.

above left Molding, cabinet knobs, and color are the unifying forces on these cabinets. Variety is shown in the placement of the knobs. The red in the Oriental area rug links the cabinets and the wood flooring.

left Glass doors break up an expanse of solid cabinetry. Variety is also achieved by the display items. The frames of the glass doors are the same as the solid ones, creating a sense of unity.

Balance

There are two basic means of achieving visual balance—symmetry and asymmetry.

Symmetry is the most recognized type of balance. Forms of equal size and visual weight are arranged on each side of an imaginary center line. They mirror one another, communicating formality and stability. A fireplace flanked by bookcases or windows is a classic example.

Asymmetry creates visual balance by properly juxtaposing objects that vary in shape, size, and color. Asymmetry communicates openness and informality. Many kitchens are structurally asymmetrical because the placement of doors, windows, and cabinets on opposite walls do not share the exact configuration, though they may be of equal visual weight.

above right and right Symmetry and asymmetry in action. Four decorative tiles in vegetable motifs (above) are arranged to split the center line of the sink, creating classic symmetry and balance. The clock (right) defines the center of the asymmetrical arrangement on the mantel. Though they are different shapes, the relative heights of the game board and vase create visual balance.

below Centering the cooktops between the hanging cabinets and on the windows and sofa in the family area creates a perfectly symmetrical relationship between two separate spaces. Symmetry lends a comforting feeling to a space.

below The fireplace wall achieves symmetry by centering the painting between the pair of French doors and sconces. Asymmetrical elements in the space are the pendent lights in the foreground and the fixture above the dining room table.

Rhythm and Emphasis

When you think of **rhythm,** music usually comes to mind, but there is also a rhythm you take in with your eyes. And like musical rhythm, visual rhythm can vary from the simple to the complex.

   Emphasis occurs when one element takes on more importance than other elements. For example, a hood with an unusual shape or made from a striking material may stand out among a wall of appliances. A focal-point wall has a color or decorative paint treatment different from other solid-color walls. A stone fireplace may dominate a dining or sitting area in an open kitchen, spotlighting that particular space.

right Flooring with strong variations in color and grain creates a vibrant visual rhythm that is matched by the equally strong grain of the cabinets. Both the flooring and cabinets are made of hickory.

left Rhythm and emphasis are evident in this contemporary kitchen. Color, shape, and line work together to create a sense of movement. The yellow column that rises from the breakfast bar draws the eye toward the white soffit that breaks up the line of the vaulted ceiling. The ceiling in turn frames the working area of the kitchen behind it. A still life sporting black, red, yellow, green, and white colors makes a dramatic statement. Its horizontal shape squares off against the vertical lines of the adjacent doorway.

Function

All designers need to think through practical details when creating a kitchen. Brainstorming about style is fun, but a beautiful kitchen that doesn't function well is a waste of time and money. It's also a disappointing reminder of what might have been if the proper attention had been paid to functionality.

A functional kitchen evolves from an organized process of reviewing practical considerations based on the concept of the work triangle as conceived by the NKBA (National Kitchen and Bath Association). You'll learn how to integrate the cook's movement and family traffic patterns; the placement of sinks, appliances, and areas for food preparation, cooking, cleanup, and dining; and other activities. These guidelines will help you combine style and function into a safe, comfortable, efficient, and beautiful kitchen.

above Just as the fireplace was the kitchen's focal point 100 years ago, the stove or cooktop is the heart of today's kitchen. Whatever powers the stove, it must be functional, efficient, and serve your family's needs.

use your RESOURCES

Return to these pages on functionality and use them as references and resources as you finalize the plans for your new kitchen. They will be especially useful as you review the planning section in Chapter 3 and the shopping guide in Chapter 4.

right Kitchen sinks are in use almost constantly and serve a multitude of functions in a modern home. This stainless-steel, double-bowl sink is deep enough to hold cooking pots, and the faucet spout doubles as a sprayer when removed from the base.

The Work Triangle

above This kitchen represents a basic work triangle with adjustments for modern kitchen use. The island with its prep sink, the main sink, and the range are the points of the triangle. The island also contains additional counter space to provide seating for family and guests.

More than 50 years ago, the work triangle was devised as a way to efficiently connect the cooktop, refrigerator, and sink. The premise was to reduce the number of steps the cook had to take in meal preparation, cooking, and cleanup. At that time most kitchens were closed-off rooms, inhabited primarily by a busy but lonely cook. The rest of the family was encouraged to stay out.

The work triangle is still a basic design and planning tool, but today's kitchens see a whole different style of food preparation, entertaining, cooking, and living. Kitchens are now a whirl of activity reflecting a modern family's hectic pace.

On the following pages you'll learn about the work triangle and activity centers such as cooking, cleaning, and preparation, and you'll see how the triangle is applied to five basic kitchen layouts.

Then in Chapter 2 you'll take a photographic journey through seven efficient and beautiful kitchens to see inspiring real-life applications of the basic principles of design and function at work.

In Chapter 3 you'll put what you've learned to work by answering a series of questions about how you and your family plan to use your new kitchen. Once you've settled on the answers, you'll begin to place major appliances and fixtures in the space and surround them with cabinets and storage, following the principles of the work triangle.

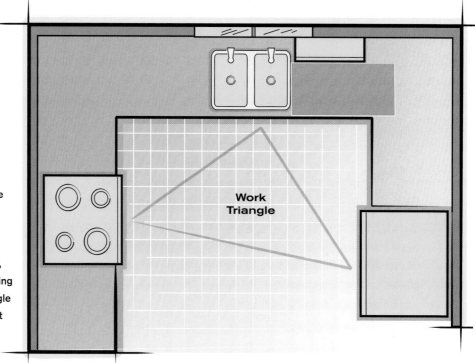

right This illustration represents the work triangle in a basic kitchen layout. Each point ends at one of the kitchen's major work centers—the sink, the stove, and the refrigerator. Arranging the work centers as a triangle allows for easy and efficient movement from one center to another.

Work Triangle

NKBA Layout Guidelines

The NKBA's guidelines reflect today's changing families' needs. The work triangle and the kitchen planning standards have been modified to include more appliances, such as the microwave oven, multiple cooks in the kitchen, and additional kitchen activity centers for computers and entertaining.

How should the triangle be arranged?

- The preferred configuration is to place the primary kitchen sink opposite the refrigerator and the primary cooking surface (often a range).

What if a kitchen is too small?

- In a one-wall kitchen or a similar tight space, the sink should be between the refrigerator and the range.

How big should the triangle be?

- Measure the distance of each of the three legs of the triangle.
- No single leg should be shorter than 4 feet or longer than 9 feet.
- When you add the three distances together, the total should be 26 feet or less.

What if a family has two cooks?

- If multiple cooks will be working simultaneously, each should have a separate work triangle. The triangles may share a leg, but should not cross over one another.
- In multiple-cook kitchens, appliances may be shared. For many it works best to share the refrigerator. A separate sink isn't a necessity, but it's a plus.
- No major traffic patterns should cut through the work triangle.
- The work triangle should not intersect an island or peninsula by any more than 12 inches.

What About Easy Access?

- Each doorway should be at least 32 inches wide and no more than 24 inches deep in the direction of travel.
- If a doorway is flanked on either side by counters, measure the minimum 32-inch clearance from the point of one counter to the closest point of the opposite counter.
- Walkways should be at least 36 inches wide.
- Work aisles, passageways between work counters and appliances, should be at least 42 inches wide. In a multiple-cook kitchen, this recommendation increases to a minimum of 48 inches.
- Ensure that no entry, appliance, or cabinet door interferes with another entry, appliance, or door.

Activity Centers

Almost as important as the work triangle are activity centers. These interrelated work centers should be designed to suit your specific space, wants, and needs. At the same time, they should make cooking, serving your family and guests, dining together, cleanup, and other activities easier to accomplish and more enjoyable.

Food Preparation Center

The food preparation center should be functional for cooking big family dinners and preparing for parties, as well as for providing easy access space for whipping up quick weeknight meals, making snacks, and zapping leftovers. This center is great for storing canned and dry goods, baking dishes, mixing bowls, can openers, storage containers, and other small appliances.

Many cooks agree that time and effort can be minimized by organizing a kitchen in such a way that ingredients, utensils, and cookware needed for favorite and often-prepared dishes are readily accessible. Plan your design so the kitchen accommodates your special culinary talents and interests. Most cooks find it sensible to store some frequently used items, such as paring knives and spices, in more than one location in the kitchen.

When preparing a meal you also need easy access to a sink for washing vegetables and filling pots with water. A pot-filler faucet mounted at the cooktop is a great feature to consider if you often find yourself lugging large pots of water from the sink to the cooktop. A secondary sink and its adjoining counter space may be the perfect spot for washing and chopping vegetables.

Subcenters

Many of today's great family kitchens have subcenters in the food preparation center, such as:

- **The food-storage center.** This is most often a pantry or a wall cabinet either in or right next to the food preparation center.
- **The snack center.** This often includes an undercounter mini fridge, a microwave oven, and a kid-friendly snack area; there might also be a second sink.
- **The breakfast center.** This might be a place near the breakfast dining area where you store quick and easy breakfast foods, bowls, and juice glasses for fix-it-yourself mornings on the go.

right The food preparation center should be located near the sink and the dishwasher to facilitate cleaning of foods and easy removal of scraps.

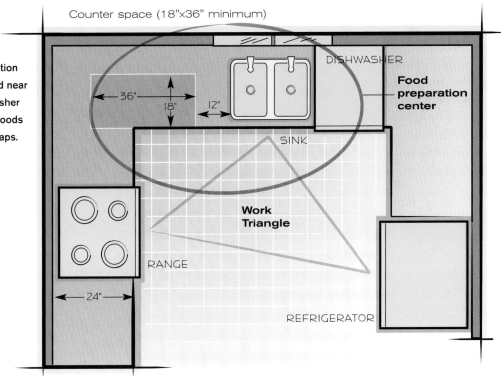

Cooking Center

An efficient layout is a critical component of the ever-busy cooking center. The cooking center consists of the cooktop or range and the microwave oven. Stand-alone ovens are typically used less often, so they can be placed outside the work triangle. If space is tight consider a range in place of a separate cooktop and oven.

A good ventilation system is also a major component of the cooking center. Ventilation systems not only play an important functional role in the kitchen, but can also make a major decorative statement. The selected system should have a fan rated at a minimum of 150 cubic feet per minute (cfm). If you have a commercial-style range, or do heavy frying or other cooking, opt for a vented model with more power.

What else should be in the cooking center? Most cooks like to have quick access to pots and pans, utensils, hot pads, spices, cooking oils, herbs, and seasonings. Locating favorite cookbooks either in the center or close by is also helpful. If you are looking for extra features, consider warming drawers. Cooks who serve large families and entertain on a regular basis often rate these as a key feature.

If you have adequate space, consider installing one microwave in the core work/cooking center and a secondary microwave oven either near the refrigerator or in the snack area. Some high-end microwaves also serve as convection ovens.

common sense STORAGE

- Keep food and other often-used items as close as possible to the relevant appliance or the area where you will use them.
- Store food in cabinets attached to cool outside walls or near shaded windows. Avoid placing cabinets near the dishwasher, oven, refrigerator, and warm exterior walls.
- Spices and cooking oils should be within easy reach of the cooktop.
- Store frequently used items within easy reach. Store less-used ones in the back of a cabinet or up high.
- Having a lower height section of countertop is helpful for chopping and other prep work, and it also gives the kids an easy place to prepare a quick snack.
- An island equipped with a sink is a useful prep center.

right The cooking center is the area immediately around the oven or cooktop. Counter surfaces should be able to withstand potential damage from hot pots and pans. There should be 9 to 15 inches minimum on each side of the cooktop.

Cleanup Center

The sink, a key feature of the work triangle, also plays a major role in the cleanup center, food preparation center, and the cooking center. Other important features of the cleanup center are the dishwasher; garbage disposer; trash and recycling containers; and adequate, easy-to-reach storage for dish towels, sponges, dishwashing detergent, and other cleaning products.

Dishwashers should be placed next to the sink on whichever side works best for the primary cook. It's also useful to have the trash container close at hand. This cuts down on the number of cleanup steps; just take the dishes to the sink, scrape, rinse if needed, and load right into the dishwasher. If you entertain frequently, you may find having two dishwashers a real timesaver. In that case consider having the dishwashers on either side of the sink or placing the second dishwasher in an island near a secondary sink.

Dining Center

Carving out the dining area creates the perfect environment for informal yet intimate gatherings. One key to successful planning is striving for convenience by locating the eating area close to the hardworking sections of the kitchen. Remember to include plenty of natural light when designing the space.

The traditional kitchen table with chairs may still be the best choice for many families, but it does require more total floor space than other options. Other popular alternatives include an island or peninsula with stools. Booths and banquettes are more conducive to intimate conversation than countertops. They typically require less clear area than a freestanding table and chairs, but more than an island or peninsula. Booths or window-seat dining can also provide extra storage space, best designated for seldom-used kitchen equipment or seasonal items.

NKBA Guidelines for the Dining Area

■ Is there a walkway behind the seated diner?

If no, the guideline is to leave at least 36 inches of floor clearance measured from the counter or table edge to any wall or other obstruction behind it.

If yes, the guideline is to leave at least 65 inches of floor clearance, including the walkway, between the seating area and any wall or other obstruction behind it.

■ For 30-inch-high tables and "eat-at" counters, allow a 30×19-inch space for each seated diner. Also allow 19 inches of clear knee space.

■ For 36-inch-high counters, allow a 24×15-inch space for each seated diner. Also allow at least 15 inches of clear knee space.

■ For 42-inch-high counters, allow a 24×12-inch space for each seated diner. Also allow at least 12 inches of clear knee space. In addition, if a place setting is to be set for dinner, a space of 24×18 inches is required for

left The cleanup center should be located next to the sink and either above or next to the dishwasher. Garbage and recycling containers should be easily accessible.

above A well-situated planning and communications center is part of the kitchen but well outside the work triangle.

Planning and Communications Center

Everyone longs to be organized. Even if you fall short of this ambitious goal, you still need a designated space to pay bills, organize mail, make phone calls, write letters, update your calendar, plan meals, and perhaps work, read, or use a desktop or laptop computer. With today's families spending more and more of their at-home time in the kitchen, many are finding the need to tuck a planning center into the allotted space.

Keys to a Useful Planning Center

- Start by making sure your mini office is located well outside the work triangle.
- When designing the space, including a separate desk with plenty of storage is a must.
- Minimum recommended desktop size is 24 inches wide and 20 inches deep, and standard desktop height is 30 inches. Allow for at least 30 inches of clearance for pulling out the desk chair.
- Everyone can use built-in file cabinets and drawers. While you are at it, designate a spot for the kids' homework and supplies.
- You might want to include a family message board or bulletin board or perhaps baskets for each family member's paperwork.

- The planning center is a convenient spot to include a shelf for favorite cookbooks.
- Some people like an adjustable, office-style chair, while others go for a stool that can be tucked under the desk when not in use.
- The space can be large or small—whatever works best for you.

Specialized Work Centers

When planning your kitchen reflect on the many activities, from cooking to working to socializing, that take place in your kitchen, and gear specific areas of the kitchen to those activities or other special interests. For example, if you or other cooks in your family love to bake, design an area that will conveniently house all your baking supplies and cookware, and consider installing a cool marble countertop, which is perfect for rolling out pastries. If possible, this counter space area should be at least 36 uninterrupted inches, and you should consider making this section of your counter a little lower than standard, for greater comfort when rolling out dough.

Would you enjoy a coffee or beverage center? If you frequently entertain, you could scope out a spot outside the main work triangle and design an area with a second sink, a small refrigerator, a separate icemaker, a wine cooler, and perhaps a mini media center.

If you have pets, consider installing a pet feeding station into a lower drawer in the kitchen. If you want to do chores like ironing near other activity centers, consider installing a pullout or fold-down ironing board, which disappears when not in use.

If you have space for a keeping room or other area with a fireplace, you will be able to capture and savor that precious moment of relaxing in front of a fire, sipping your morning coffee before heading out for the mad rush of the day.

If your children do their homework in the kitchen, make sure you include a place for their supplies and other often-needed items, such as a dictionary. Gardening and potting lovers should plan for a special nook for themselves. Keep everything you need for gardening in a handy spot so you can sneak in your hobby during any spare moment. You might also consider a crafts center for you and your kids or a place for a sewing machine and other mending supplies.

Today's kitchen truly is the center of the home. The key is to make it accessible, open, light, friendly, and efficient. Weighing options before you begin your remodeling job will only increase your enjoyment later.

Basic Kitchen Layouts

Whether you are planning a simple facelift or a major remodeling, your goal should be a design that gives you the largest and most functional area of work and storage space possible while creating a look that is open, light, and aesthetically pleasing to you.

Kitchens come in all shapes and sizes. Your choice of layout will probably be determined by the size and configuration of your available space. The following layouts, ranging from the single wall or galley to the larger open plan and including the L-, U-, and G-shapes, each have advantages and disadvantages. They are all based on efficient arrangements of fixtures and appliances that create effective work triangles and adequate storage. Use these ideas as a starting point to design the kitchen that works best for you and your family.

below right Space is compressed in a galley arrangement and is most efficient when the sink is placed between the stove and refrigerator on the opposite counter.

below Galley or single-wall kitchens can have efficient work spaces if appliances and fixtures are laid out to offer the maximum amount of counter space and if adequate storage for utensils and portable appliances is provided.

Single-Wall or Galley Kitchen

Two layout options for tight, narrow spaces often found in small or older homes or apartments are single-wall or galley kitchens. If a **single-wall** kitchen, where the refrigerator, stove, and sink are placed along one wall is the best choice, put the sink in the center and the refrigerator and stove on opposite ends to maximize counter space. Make sure the refrigerator hinges on the side away from the sink so the door won't open into your limited work space. Allow for 4 feet of counter space on either side of the sink and a space between 9 and 15 inches minimum for the range.

The **galley** kitchen (often called a two-wall or corridor kitchen) is more efficient than the single-wall option because it offers more counter and storage space. One design option places the sink and refrigerator on one wall and centers the cooktop between them on the opposite wall. The other places the sink on one wall and the stove and refrigerator on the other. You need at least 4 feet of clear floor space between the counters. Try to avoid traffic patterns that cut through this tight work space. While space is limited many cooks actually find the galley layout easy to use.

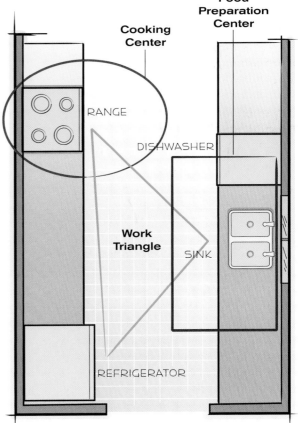

U-Shape Kitchen

To allow for at least 4 feet of work space in the center of the kitchen, a U-shape kitchen requires an interior space of at least 8×8 feet. Many designers consider the U-shape to be the most efficient and versatile kitchen configuration. This popular layout allows for storage and counter space on three sides. It works best if each of the three walls hosts one of the three elements of the work triangle: the refrigerator, the sink, and the cooktop. Another advantage to this dead-end design is that it naturally cuts down on traffic interference. Be careful not to make the kitchen or the work triangle too large, or you will end up out of breath as you jog through the kitchen from point to point.

If you have a larger space, an island can house the cooktop or a sink, reducing the size of the work triangle but allowing room for many of the specialized centers desired by today's homeowners. U-shaped kitchens, especially those with small footprints, are not ideal for use by two cooks.

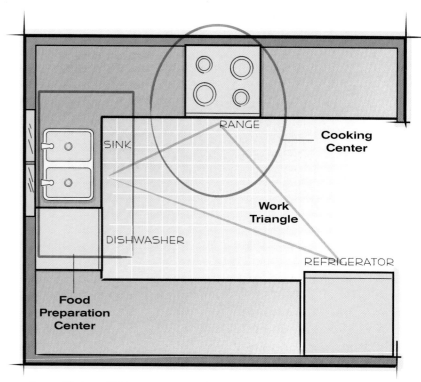

above U-shape kitchens are extremely efficient, using available space effectively to create easy preparation and cooking flows. The minimum interior space should be 8×8 feet.

L-Shape Kitchen

The L-shape design works in kitchens with two adjacent walls. It requires less space than the U-shape kitchen, but it can be almost as efficient. The better L designs keep the triangle and other major work centers close to the crook of the L. A popular configuration is to have the refrigerator and the sink on one wall and the cooktop on the adjoining wall. This conserves steps, accommodates a logical work flow, and results in the most efficient placement of the elements. Traffic cutting through the triangle is typically not a problem with this layout.

An L-shape kitchen with an island makes it easier for more than one cook to be working simultaneously, adds more storage and counter space, and can be designed for a snack bar or countertop dining area.

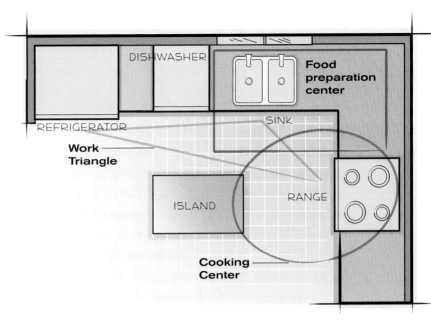

above L-shape kitchens can be almost as efficient as U-shapes and offer smooth traffic patterns through the space.

above An L-shape kitchen focuses the working space on two walls, but an island adds flexibility and allows for more fluid movement in the space.

island **MAGIC**

- Islands can be a key component in many kinds of layouts and should be placed to enhance the efficiency and workflow of the kitchen.
- They can house a cooktop or a secondary sink where a cook or helper can wash vegetables or fill pots with water. Other options include tucking a second dishwasher or small refrigerator in a handy spot in your island.
- They can serve as snack bars, or you can design a lower-level island (at a standard table height of 30 inches) to accommodate regular dining chairs.
- Islands are the perfect place for a small amount of the more expensive make-a-statement surface that will give your kitchen that needed pizzazz.
- Remember to include electrical outlets in your island. Keep in mind that costs may increase if you choose to install a cooktop or sink with added plumbing and ventilation factors.
- Give yourself enough space. When including an island in your plans, remember that the recommended minimum work aisle clearances of 42 inches should be planned for all sides of the island.

G-Shape Kitchen

Rather than incorporating an island, the G-shape kitchen houses a peninsula. The versatile peninsula can serve many of the same purposes as an island, but it typically takes up less floor space and anchors to a wall or line of cabinets rather than being freestanding. The G-shape kitchen usually requires a larger area with one section similar to the L-shape kitchens and the other section identified by the peninsula. In this layout a peninsula with pullout stools provides a great gathering place for friends and family while keeping them out of the cook's way. This configuration also offers additional storage and counter space.

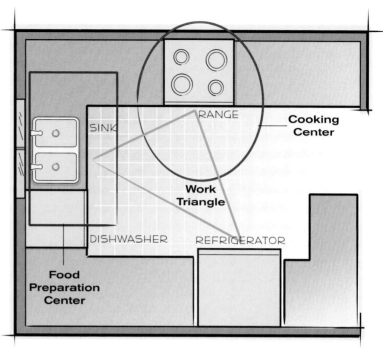

above right and below A G-shape kitchen incorporates a peninsula as extra counter or dining space. The work triangle is similar to the U-shape arrangement.

Open-Plan Kitchen

The open-plan kitchen is a common layout in many modern homes where there are no walls between the kitchen and the family room. Family members and guests treat the spaces as one, and flow freely from area to area. This arrangement further magnifies the trend of the kitchen as the family gathering spot. The kitchen itself can be many of the configurations previously described with some sort of definition dividing the kitchen space from the great-room or family room. Hanging suspended cabinetry or installing a pot rack over a counter are examples of ways to define the two spaces without an actual wall or barrier.

right and below Two examples show how open-plan kitchens flow easily from one space to another. Transitions from one area to another can be defined by changes in flooring materials, such as the move from ceramic tile to wood strip flooring to and area rug as shown below.

CHAPTER 2

Inspiring
Designs

Your dream kitchen starts with personal inspiration and becomes real by searching out concrete ideas. Studying style and function, and the details of each, provides you with almost limitless possibilities.

Some kitchens are ideal for serving a small family, while others handily accommodate numerous guests. Some kitchens manage to do both by anchoring open spaces shared with a dining area and a great-room. Whatever style and size kitchen you choose, it must work as part of a whole. It must serve as a complement to the areas that surround it and integrate itself easily into the overall design concept.

On the following pages you'll explore seven inspired kitchens to help you discover your own design solutions. Each of these kitchens is a balance of style and function—they are beautiful, and they work.

CHAPTER 2 CONTENTS

left Many elements must come together to create a great kitchen. An overall design first and foremost makes efficient use of the space, but also important are adequate storage, good transitions between rooms, and well-located serving and eating areas.

Warming up the view from the kitchen, a stone fireplace and hot-chocolate-tone walls lend texture and color. The cabinets flanking the fireplace match those in the kitchen, but are stained and varnished instead of being painted.

Old-World
Flavors

This kitchen was a relic of the early 1990s before a makeover warmed its all-white cabinets and walls.

The kitchen in this spacious home defies traditional thinking about what constitutes an ideal floor plan. The unusual arrangement is comparable to a theater-in-the-round, with the kitchen being center stage. Wrapped on three sides by a living room, casual sitting area, and dining room, the kitchen more than holds its own when it comes to convenience and space.

The central island divides the kitchen into zones, with the sink and cooktop on one side, and a wet bar area on the other. On the cook's side of the island, large items find a home in the spacious base cabinet that forms the island, and a pair of drawers hold small utensils. Electrical receptacles are plentiful and convenient for plugging in mixers and blenders. The island itself functions as a breakfast bar, a buffet server, a worktable, and an additional food preparation center. It's also a popular gathering spot for family and guests.

From early in the morning until homework is finished by bedtime, the kitchen fulfills the needs of five active children and their parents.

Space and Light

The cook has unobstructed movement between the sink and stove. Sleek black appliances—a large double oven and a side-by-side refrigerator—recess into the floor-to-ceiling wall of cupboards.

In any kitchen, lighting is of paramount importance. Adequate task lighting is essential for food preparation and cooking, while multiple sources of ambient light are highly desirable. Upper cabinets above the sink and cooktop are placed high enough to allow in natural light from windows in the sitting room. Soffits rimming the kitchen on all sides contain recessed lighting canisters, as does the ceiling. They're carefully positioned to illuminate counters and opened cabinets. A fan with a light fixture brightens the central island for eating or homework.

Light-color surfaces provide maximum reflectivity. The ceiling is classic white. Honey-tone glaze on the cabinet doors accentuates the rectangular contours of the raised paneling. The glaze was also applied to the island's beadboard side and paneled doors and drawers. The solid-surfacing countertops, once edged with a golden band of shiny metal, were updated with a softer painted edging, highlighted with the glaze used on the cabinets.

above While working at the sink, cooks can enjoy an unbroken view of the outdoors. State-of-the-art fixtures include an aerator, a spray hose with a brush that pulls out from the faucet, and a separate faucet for filtered water. A single lever on the main faucet allows one-handed temperature adjustment of hot and cold water.

above The black-glass cooktop, which matches other appliances in the room, is hidden from view by the raised portion of the counter that divides the two rooms and is useful for display.

below Upper cabinets hang from the soffit, with openings over two main work centers: the sink and the cooktop. Above the cooktop, cabinets have glass doors on both sides to let sunlight through. Several people can gather at the island for conversation, coffee, or a meal. The island's expansive countertop also functions as a serving table or work surface.

above A wet bar tucked into the corner offers convenient for serving drinks at parties, and guests remain slightly away from other kitchen activities. Glass-front cabinet doors protect crystal and other favorite items from dust without covering them up.

above A pantry cupboard, lined with shelves and a grid system on the doors provides valuable storage.

left Large items find a home in the spacious base cabinet that forms the island. The pair of drawers hold smaller utensils. Electrical receptacles are plentiful and convenient for plugging in mixers, blenders, or a tiny lamp for dining.

Roomy Connections

Despite its interior location, the kitchen is bright and airy, thanks to the wider than usual openings between the adjoining rooms.

A two-step change in floor level connects the kitchen and sitting room. Natural light—filtering through the undraped windows and transoms in the sitting area—floods the kitchen. The honeyed glaze used on the kitchen cabinets and island repeats in the faux finish walls of the sitting room and the two decorative columns.

right Two columns support the ceiling while creating architectural interest. Their sponged-on glaze finish harmonizes with the faux painting on the walls

above The view from the sitting room into the kitchen is delightfully unobscured with an open space topped by above-eye-level storage with glass doors in the center unit. More storage and display space is in the open shelving that backs up to the cooktop.

right Abundant sunlight pours into the kitchen by way of the sitting-room windows. The slightly raised display shelf behind the standard-height countertop keeps food preparation out of sight for guests.

As a complement to the kitchen and sitting room, deep-tone color defines the living room, which has a striking fireplace surround. The vaulted ceiling as well as windows and transoms contribute to the kitchen's spaciousness. Sconces placed high above the fireplace draw the eye upward.

right Matching candlesticks frame the metal sculpture in the center of the mantel and reinforce the sense of symmetry present along the entire wall.

below Textured paint finishes on the columns and cabinets lend a European touch to an open kitchen that serves a busy family. The beaded paneling has the same gold-tone glaze used on all the kitchen cabinets.

Multipurpose Dining Room

The dining room is on the same floor level as the kitchen and shares the same cabinetry, although in a different finish. Glazed walls unite it visually with the kitchen and sitting room.

Furnishings in the dining room have a casual appeal, contrasting pleasantly with the formal lines of the columns. Ladder-back chairs with rush seats, a sturdy dining table, and a pie safe add character.

The dining room storage unit, which also serves as a desk and buffet table, matches the kitchen cabinets. This arrangement demonstrates how a home office can have dual functions. Tucked away from the sitting room and kitchen where the family tends to congregate, the desk gives either parent a quiet place to pay bills, write a grocery list, or plan a party.

Surrounded by sunny dining, sitting, and living rooms, this bright kitchen lives large.

right Two steps provide a gentle change in elevation between the dining room and sitting room.

below A multicolored area rug in the dining room creates a focal point, separating the table and chairs from the rest of the space.

Hardware on the upper cabinets *(above left)* differs in shape from the base-cabinet knobs *(below)*. Round on the bottom cabinets, but oblong on the top, the cast-metal pulls have the same old-world-iron finish. Using different styles of drawer pulls adds interest to the doors and is one of the latest trends in cabinetry.

above Angled at one end of the dining room, the home office has plenty of drawers, cabinets, and cubbyholes to store dishes, financial records, recipes, and school supplies.

A U-shape kitchen is an ideal choice for an open space such as a loft, where living and working areas are defined not so much by walls as by groupings of elements. The U-shape clearly differentiates the working area of the kitchen from the rest of the space.

Lofty
Inspiration

Art is at the heart of this loft, where a professional and personal way of being blends with an expression of kitchen comfort. Whether set up for everyday meals or lavish entertaining, the kitchen inspires the resident artist to play chef.

L oft living is enjoying a renaissance—and with good reason. Located in a renovated ice cream manufacturing plant, this loft is within walking distance of theaters, museums, restaurants, a river walk, and the lake. A loft space is the ideal location for homeowners interested in city life.

The kitchen blends effortlessly into the open space. Tucked to one side of the dining area on the loft's expansive maple floor, the kitchen is compact and efficient. Its dark appliances and sunlit maple cabinetry balance the loft's whitewashed brick walls.

Designed to accommodate a creative cook, the kitchen's U-shape directs traffic outside its self-contained work area and encourages frequent guests and helpers to congregate around the raised bar at the kitchen's open end. The lower level of the countertop allows the cook to continue preparations while conversing with guests. The bar, which is home to comfortable black leather swivel stools, also serves as a buffet or serving area when extended family and guests are present, and as an informal eating area. Made of polished black granite, its sleek surface harmonizes quietly with the loft's eclectic mix of tones and textures.

Cozy Kitchen

Used on adjoining countertops, the smooth granite surface eases meal prep and cleanup. The maple cabinets, including wine bottle cubbies, wrap around two walls, providing plenty of storage.

A lower—albeit 12-foot—ceiling in the kitchen gives the area an intimate feel, and lighting contributes to both warmth and function. Because the kitchen is situated on the loft's internal wall, the ceiling has sufficient recessed canned fixtures to provide ambient light to the work area. Underneath the cabinetry, task lighting illuminates the countertop for food-prep chores. Adding to the warmth are the kitchen's walls, which take their color cue from the loft's terra-cotta-tone interior walls. Here, a darker latte color gives the space its own identity.

At the end of the cabinet run, a bank of display shelves show off stemware, while several lacy white candelabras, brought home as mementos from a family wedding, grace the area above the cabinetry.

right Display shelves angled at the end of the upper cabinetry soften the sharp corners while providing open storage for glassware.

below Smooth black countertops suit the sleek urban setting, with the granite surface providing enduring good looks.

left A stainless-steel, double-bowl sink and retractable spray faucet aid meal prep and cleanup chores. The asymmetrical shape of the sink adds interest.

above Like the other appliances, the black gas range and hood contrast with the maple cabinets.

right Black appliances, including refrigerator and dishwasher, blend with the glossy countertops.

above Roll-out shelving puts large pots, pans, and mixing bowls within immediate reach.

Simplicity Rules

Throughout the living space, simplicity reigns. Light maple floors stretch from one end of the loft to the other, and living and dining areas are defined by plush area rugs in teal, terra-cotta, sage green, and claret red. Terra-cotta walls echo the color of surrounding rooftops, and a maple mantel that matches the floors encloses a corner gas fireplace. Mexican folk art and a personal painting adorn the mantel. A soft, overstuffed claret sofa and leather lounging chair cozy up to the warm wood entertainment armoire. A wooden heirloom table—home to a collection of family photographs—brings warmth to a white brick wall, and an unobtrusive sound system pipes soft music throughout the space.

In the dining area an oval dining table is layered in claret linen, old lace, and a tasseled topper, and maple chairs are cushioned in taupe suede. Then there are the final artistic touches—what the homeowner dubs "urban artifacts"—a wicker mannequin draped in a sheer, beaded scarf, an antique trunk that stores holiday ornaments, simple stacking tables, an oversize mirror framed in ceiling tin, and window-side greenery cascading over its perch on a Roman pedestal.

above A roomy closet, equipped with floor-to-ceiling wire shelving, offers more storage.

above Comfortable stools pull up for breakfast or as extra seating during a party. Above the bar and throughout the loft, pendent lighting descends from overhead tracks, giving the space a glow after nightfall.

left An eclectic mix of furnishings creates a distinctive flavor. The copy of the Mona Lisa portrait juxtaposed next to a wicker mannequin exhibits uninhibited decorating flair.

above Beyond the dining room, double doors discreetly close off the artist's studio.

below Night never swallows a city skyline. Canister-like porch lights beckon guests outside for a view that becomes spectacular as the sun sinks.

above Exposed ceilings and walls enhance the elegantly simple industrial lines of the loft. Thrown open, the double doors invite guests into the studio. The partial wall separates living and work areas, yet keeps light from being blocked when the artist is at work.

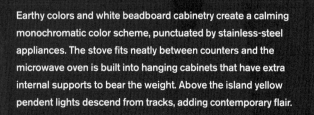

Earthy colors and white beadboard cabinetry create a calming monochromatic color scheme, punctuated by stainless-steel appliances. The stove fits neatly between counters and the microwave oven is built into hanging cabinets that have extra internal supports to bear the weight. Above the island yellow pendent lights descend from tracks, adding contemporary flair.

Streamlined Country Comfort

Country style dominates this L-shape kitchen anchored by a central island used for work and relaxation.

An uncluttered look becomes today's country style, as exemplified by this kitchen's clean lines. Two walls of cabinets with drawer space, above and below the countertops, offer plenty of storage so that textured ceramic tile can remain beautifully exposed. The basic layout is an L-shape with a central island. The two-level island, complete with a wraparound higher tier and a ceramic sink, is surrounded by 4½ feet of space on either side. This generous passage arrangement allows a single cook to move easily from one workstation to another and also provides adequate space for several kitchen workers.

Although spacious enough to accommodate a number of guests, the kitchen has a cozy feel. White beadboard cabinets, laminated cypress flooring, and cinnamon brown walls keep the look comfortable and casual. The symmetrical arrangement of the cabinetry that surrounds the stove also creates a comfortable feeling. An oak table and black lacquered chairs in the dining area reinforce the low-key atmosphere.

Convivial Space

The design of this kitchen demonstrates how an island can open up an L-shape layout. Wider than normal walkways keep traffic running smoothly. The island is accessible, even when the dishwasher and oven doors are open. An island sink—smartly situated so that it doesn't back into the primary sink and food-prep area—enables a second cook to pitch in with chores, such as rinsing and chopping vegetables. Family members can sit on stools and chat without interrupting meal preparation.

While the island serves as the central gathering place, work spaces around the kitchen perimeter are convenient. A dishwasher, double-bowl ceramic sink, and brushed nickel gooseneck faucet make cleanup easy, as do nearby pullout waste and recycling bins. A microwave oven has a niche near the dining table so family members can quickly zap popcorn for a snack or heat up leftovers for lunch.

below Pairs of Roman columns rising from low dividers mark the transition from the kitchen to the great-room. The open space facilitates circulation when company mingles. In the kitchen a built-in bar to the right of the kitchen island houses stemware and functions as a place to serve beverages. A rag-rolled paint finish of softly melded beige and coffee tones sets off the bar, while complementing the rich, dark brown color of the other walls.

above Curved entrances lead to the heart of the home.

above A multiglobed chandelier casts a soft light during family meals. Mixing and matching furniture as shown above is a hallmark of country style.

above In the spirit of streamlined country style, decorative touches are minimal. The dishwasher has a recessed paneled beadboard front so that it blends in with other cabinetry.

below A secondary sink, ample storage, and a long stretch of countertop allow the island to function as additional work space. Open baskets house school supplies, coloring books, and crayons, so children can amuse themselves or do homework at the kitchen table.

above The secondary sink's brushed nickel fixtures match those of the primary sink.

Storage Galore

The cooking area dominates the second wall of the L-layout, with plenty of nearby storage. Just to the left of the range, an upper cabinet door contains spices in bins. Because the island offers roomy work space, four upper wall cabinets extend to the countertop, providing storage cubbies for dish towels, utensils, and gadgets. Undercounter cabinetry features roll-out shelves.

above Watered-glass cabinetry doors above the range and brushed nickel pulls complement the stainless steel. While glass doors offer display options, they will require frequent cleaning when placed above a range as will the storage shelf.

above Wicker baskets slide easily in and out of open cabinets. Baskets provide great storage for vegetables as well as kitchen utensils and linens.

right The cooking station boasts plenty of counter space on either side of the gas range.

right On the end of the island near the range, roll-out shelves hold pots and pans, while drawers store cooking utensils.

above Snug drawers outfitted with old-fashioned pulls hold dish towels and other supplies. The drawers are within easy reach of both the primary sink and the range.

above To the immediate left of the range, an upper cabinet door swings open to reveal spices aligned in bins.

Friendly Ambience

Lighting throughout the kitchen enhances the well-planned design. Recessed lights illuminate areas throughout. Task lighting installed under upper cabinets facilitates food prep and cooking. When the family entertains, lighting above upper cabinets and below cabinets at floor level cultivates the festive mood. In this atmosphere guests truly enjoy all the comforts of home.

right At night ambient lighting accents warm the kitchen, creating a cozy and comfortable atmosphere.

This unfettered kitchen keeps within the simplicity of the house's Cape Cod architecture. It does, however, depart from the materials often used in a Cape Cod kitchen, including laminate or soapstone countertops, stained oak or maple wood, and ceramic tile. Instead it uses hickory on the cabinets and floor and granite on the countertops.

Refined Rustic

Wood, natural light, and clean lines catch the eye, but this carefully planned design ensures comfort and ease of movement.

Simplicity reigns in this lakeside kitchen, which takes its inspiration from Cape Cod style. Small, symmetrical houses typify this type of architecture, which dates from the early colonial period. The no-nonsense L-shape layout is devoid of complicated patterns, textures, or colors.

The choice of natural materials reinforces the kitchen's straightforward beauty. Hickory, the only wood, graces the floor, as well as the beadboard cabinets and island. Granite, the only countertop surface, also emphasizes the uncluttered look.

The walls, painted butter cream throughout, are subdued when compared with the wood. The plaster ceiling, with its tray dropped only a few inches, is equally subtle. The appliances are white because function, not an attention-getting trendy look, serves as their primary role.

Light streams through unadorned casement windows, allowing views of trees and birds from the double sink. Window treatments are unnecessary, as the bare windows and stained mullions and muntins are framed in crisp white. A soft glow from recessed cans in the ceiling and traditional lighting fixtures augment the natural light.

Easy Transitions

The traffic path behind the island accesses the living room and hall so the family can cut through the kitchen without walking far or interrupting the cook. (See photograph below center.)Ease of movement and comfort continue into other areas. The rail on the staircase, for instance, is grooved and narrow for easy grasping.

Flooring, too, is vital to comfort. Although handsome ceramic tile might complement the cabinets in this kitchen, it would be hard on feet. In contrast, hickory is a softer surface. This wood needs only little care; mopping can require only a simple mixture of vinegar and water. Hickory will endure as long as it is sealed with polyurethane every other year and protected from long exposure to moisture, such as spills.

This kitchen offers adequate room to maneuver without wasting space. For example, traffic space on every side of the island is 4 feet wide. The cook can open the oven door or the dishwasher drawers without backing into the island.

above Wooden steps provide the transition between the kitchen and a hallway. Notice the bullnose trim that finishes the line between the step and the wall.

right The island and the square doorway accessing the living room repeat the kitchen's horizontal and vertical lines. The frame of the doorway, salvaged from a 125-year-old barn, adds textural interest.

below Floating shelves catch the eye on the way into the kitchen. Family photographs displayed as a collection provide a sense of history.

right This bar sink is small, in keeping with the scale of the island. Family members can use it to wash their hands without disturbing the cook. The sink is also handy for simple prep work or pleasant activities, such as arranging flowers.

above The lighting fixture above the sink contributes old-fashioned flavor, complementing the traditional sink fixtures. The brushed nickel finish provides warmth and texture.

above The range's smooth ceramic surface is even with the granite countertop, which allows the cook to slide a hot skillet instead of lifting it. The top oven accommodates daily use and the second oven comes in handy when the cook is preparing large meals.

Practical Island Beauty

The island itself provides sufficient knee space so that even taller family members can perch on stools and cross their legs. Instead of lining up on one side, the stools face one another, allowing for eye contact and friendly conversation without forcing people to turn their heads or lean forward awkwardly. What is more, the cook does not become the object of a spectator sport, with a row of people watching a flurry of activity.

To prevent sharp edges, the granite surface is double-beveled, just like the other countertops. Clipped corners also soften the lines.

The pendent lights bathe the granite without creating reflective glare. Whatever the task—cooking, paying bills, sorting mail, or helping a child with an art project—no one suffers eye strain.

For all its comfort, the island is designed for this kitchen. Instead of resembling a rectangular block, it possesses a tablelike quality, with two squared legs reminiscent of simple columns.

Handy Work Stations

This kitchen is built for entertaining, whether centered around three-generation family gatherings or an informal buffet dinner for 25 or more. With sinks, appliances, and cabinets on two adjoining walls, the L-shape layout forms a tight work triangle for efficiency. Long stretches of counter space allow the cook to move easily between work stations, even when there's another family chef involved in the action, or a few guests who need space to unpack potluck dishes.

The work space to the right of the double sink enables the cook to wash, slice, or chop various foods without feeling crowded.

above The view from the island makes prep work a pleasure. As you plan your kitchen/great-room, focus on and take advantage of exterior views.

Food-Prep Area

Today most kitchens have double sinks, but the size of each bowl may not be well-planned. In this kitchen the left-hand sink is large enough to accommodate two pots or an oversize pan that needs to soak. The other sink, though smaller, is an adequate size for the garbage disposer.

Although granite and stainless steel were initially considered for the sinks cast iron was the ultimate choice. From a design perspective the white sink echoes the appliances and the framing around the windows. Equally important, however, is the fact that cast iron offers easy cleanup and low-maintenance.

above The soap dispenser is situated above the larger sink, where it is used most frequently. The lotion dispenser and spray hose are to the right of the faucet. The smaller sink is used for rinsing foods and feeding scraps into the garbage disposer.

left Plenty of countertop space to the left of the sink adds room for food prep and cleanup. A pullout cutting board puts convenience at the cook's fingertips.

left Handy pullout storage to the left of the sink has a rack for dish towels and a shelf for cleaning supplies. A narrow bin keeps sponges and other items within easy reach.

Stretching more than 4 feet to the left of the sink and ending where the refrigerator stands, additional counter space makes an ideal location for cleanup. Here the cook can spread out to store a number of leftovers in containers. Also, dirty glassware, plates, pots, and pans have a place to sit until they can be loaded in the two-drawer dishwasher.

top left Although the garbage disposer takes up space underneath the sink, specially designed drawers allow room to stack dishtowels and other items.

below left The lowest drawer below the sink houses serving bowls used during special occasions.

below Sturdy cabinet hinges offer both strength and adjustability. Hinges should be adjustable up and down as well as in and out to ensure that doors can be leveled and lined up properly with each other.

above Sometimes homeowners create makeshift recycling centers in the cramped space underneath the kitchen sink. Plumbing fixtures and the garbage disposer make this an awkward area and reduce space for tall containers. The recycling center in this kitchen has a door front that pulls out a deep drawer with two lined receptacles the size of kitchen-size garbage containers. The location near the sink allows for quick rinsing of cans or plastic.

Health-Conscious Storage

The cabinets, arguably the strongest overall design statement in a kitchen, are a great investment. A particularly noteworthy feature is the appliance garage. The front rolls up when appliances are needed but otherwise stays down so that the kitchen stays neat.

Inside the garage are a shelf and an outlet in the granite. An appliance can be plugged in and used on the spot. In fact it's important to place outlets and switches at each workstation. Even with two cooks, no one is inconvenienced. By being positioned at counter level, this storage unit prevents unnecessary bending or reaching up for heavy appliances.

Installing drawers ensures easy access. It's wise to store items needed on a daily basis in the top drawer to minimize bending down. Stooping for cookware causes a sore back, especially if the pots and pans are heavy. They, too, belong in a top drawer. In this kitchen, drawers make up most of the cabinets. Although many conventional drawers pull out three-quarters, these are full extension so that every inch of space is reachable.

Locating utensils in a drawer as close as possible to the work space where they will be used cuts down on extra movement. For example, mixing bowls can nest in a drawer immediately below the countertop where the whisk, spoons, and other tools are clustered. The brushed-nickel pulls have a slim, traditional line. They're easy to grab and pull.

above To the left of the range, the top drawer sports a wire mesh covering. The mesh lets air circulate to prevent mold or too much moisture. This drawer is deep enough to hold seasonings or vegetable staples such as potatoes and onions. A mesh-covered drawer is also an ideal place to stash bread, crackers, fruit, pretzels, and other foods for making snacks or light lunches.

above Tall, vertical racks are large enough to store sizable casserole dishes, cookie sheets, and trays.

below It's wise to design a kitchen to avoid unnecessary actions, such as bending over, stooping, reaching deep into cupboards, and lifting heavy appliances and dishes. Deep pullout drawers throughout this kitchen have easy-to grasp hardware and extend to their full length in a single fluid motion.

above and left This appliance garage can easily accommodate four or five appliances as well as wire storage units. The front of the appliance garage rolls down so that the kitchen stays neat. It is generally recommended that microwave ovens be supported on both sides to relieve stress on the wall cabinet.

above Top cabinets with clear glass windows offer a wonderful way to display collectibles. Interior rope lighting catches the sparkle of a pitcher, goblets, and other pieces. Such lighting calls for close attention to details inside the cabinets. In this case wainscoted hickory, including the clear finish, is used just as it is on cabinet exteriors. The lighting plays up the warmth of the wood, emitting a glow just below ceiling level.

Because the homeowners did not rush into a plan, they anticipated their immediate and future needs. The nine months they devoted to reading articles and books, clipping photos, discussing style, and investigating elements were time well spent. They can look forward to spending many happy years in this sunny kitchen.

This large, open traditional-style kitchen suits the lifestyle of the homeowners, who have a young family.

Traditional Treasure

This traditional kitchen is as functional as it is beautiful. The open floor plan suits the lifestyle of a young family that enjoys entertaining and family gatherings.

In a family with young children, these homeowners chose an open floor plan that would allow them to do serious cooking while keeping an eye on the children's activities in the kitchen, the adjacent dining room, and nearby gathering room. They also wanted a kitchen that would be suitable for entertaining and large family gatherings. With these goals in mind, they worked with builders to design a spacious and hardworking kitchen. All their planning resulted in this warm and inviting traditional kitchen that features a large, conveniently arranged work area and plenty of space for children to call their own. The raised countertop along the L-shape set of base cabinets provides space for after-school snacks, homework, and games during family time. It also furnishes a place for resting drinks and hors d'oeuvre plates during festive gatherings. The center island combines the features of a hardworking food-prep area with the elegance of a formal buffet. The kitchen is also designed to open into the dining area that, in turn, opens into the gathering room—a floor plan that suits the lifestyle of this family.

Island Paradise

One particular feature the homeowners knew they wanted in their new kitchen was a center island. They consider the island the centerpiece of the room and it serves multiple functions. When cooking an elaborate meal, it serves as additional food preparation space. During holiday gatherings, the homeowners use it as a buffet server. The island's built-in bookcase provides room for cookbooks and displays decorative items. The island also houses storage enclosed behind cabinet doors and a wine cooler in which white wines are kept at optimum temperature and humidity level.

above The center island has a built-in bookcase at one end. The adjustable shelves provide storage space for cookbooks and display space for candles and other decorative items. The dark wood of the cabinetry is emphasized by the lighter color of the floor.

left and above The darker solid-surfacing countertop of the island contrasts nicely with the lighter countertops throughout the rest of the kitchen and highlights the darker gray tiles accenting the backsplash. The gas cooktop is within easy reach of the island.

left The higher counter bordering one edge of the kitchen is an ideal place for after-school snacks and homework. The location allows the homeowners to supervise children's activities while preparing dinner. The light speckled solid-surface countertop is a nice contrast to the dark finish on the cabinets and to the darker countertop on the island.

Traditional Touches

Although this kitchen serves the needs of a young family, its style nods toward the traditional. Two types of wood give this kitchen its rich good looks. The cabinets are maple with a cherry stain. The floor is cherry tongue and groove with a clear coat seal. Raised panel cabinet doors and upper cabinets topped with detailed molding add to the elegant design.

below A cove of windows in the dining area adjacent to the kitchen bathes both rooms in natural light and affords a view of the stream behind the home. Window treatments in the dining room mirror the kitchen window treatment and provide continuity in the two rooms.

Lighten Up

Lighting plays an important role in good kitchen design. When the homeowners met with the electrician to plan the lighting for this room they asked him to design the lighting scheme as if it were his own kitchen. Recessed can lights throughout the kitchen and rope lights in the upper cabinet coves offer ambient light to produce a daylight effect. Pendent lights above the island provide in-between light—task light for the island and additional ambient lighting for the kitchen. Undercabinet lights provide task lighting to work at the countertops. The result of the lighting scheme is a room with a warm, inviting overall glow and plenty of focused task lighting for each work area.

above Natural light streaming in and a deep sill on the window above the sink provide an ideal spot for plants. A simple fabric valance adorns the window while still affording a view.

above Rope lights in the coves above the cabinets add another dimension to the ambient light and fill the room with a warm glow. Cove lighting is an inexpensive and easy way to provide an additional source of light.

left Undercabinet lights provide task lighting for work at the countertops. This light source makes these work areas safer because it eliminates shadows from the work surface. Undercabinet lights should be placed where they will illuminate the work surface without shining in someone's eyes.

right Pendent lights above the island provide task lighting for the island and additional ambient lighting for the kitchen. Recessed can lights provide the main ambient lighting for the room.

above A large walk-in pantry in the kitchen and just off the entrance from the garage makes unpacking and storing groceries a snap. Top pantry shelves are a convenient place to stow seldom used yet handy small kitchen appliances.

above These shallow storage shelves are near the cooktop and ideal for housing spices, sauces, and other frequently used items. In addition to the convenience of having items close at hand, the etched cabinet door fronts provide interest on what would have otherwise been a bare wall.

Storage Solutions

The homeowners were careful to include plenty of generous storage features to make their kitchen functional as well as stylish. Base cabinets include fully extendable pull-out shelves that prevent items at the back from being forgotten. Another set of base cabinets features pull-out recycling bins and a garbage container. Positioning a large walk-in pantry in the kitchen and near the door to the garage makes it convenient for the family to unload and put away groceries. Shallow shelves near the cooktop put spices and other cooking staples within easy reach during food preparation.

above The built-in wine storage above the refrigerator is a convenient place to store bottles of red wine and a decorative element of the cabinet design. Storing wines away from the heat of the cooktop and double oven keeps vintages at their best. The wine rack is positioned several inches above the top of the refrigerator to protect it from the heat the unit emits.

left Fully extendable pull-out shelves in the base cabinets eliminate the struggle to access items stored at the back of cabinets. These full-extension slides are designed to withstand heavy use.

Kitchen Design and Planning **67**

Galley kitchens such as this one feature a tight work triangle with the stove, refrigerator, and sink in conveniently close proximity to one another. Galley kitchens also provide ample counter and storage space.

Generous Galley

Galley kitchens can provide an efficient work triangle and offer plenty of counter and storage space.

When these homeowners were in the planning stages of designing their new kitchen, they considered their lifestyle and unique needs. They wanted a kitchen that would be convenient, with plenty of storage, a layout that would contribute to speedy meal prep, and one that would offer all of this within a compact footprint.

The answer to their kitchen design needs? This hardworking galley kitchen, which the homeowners refer to as the "step-saver layout." In addition to a compact work area that makes food preparation quick and convenient, they have counter surfaces adjacent to all food preparation and cooking areas, and ample storage. This kitchen is also designed to accommodate an adult son who uses a wheelchair for mobility. The extra wide corridor allows both of them to occupy the kitchen at the same time, and it provides adequate clearance for the wheelchair, even when a drawer or cabinet is open.

left To assist the homeowner in transferring his son and wheelchair from inside the house to the garage, a programmable door opener was installed. This push button, located in the kitchen along the backsplash, opens the door between the kitchen and garage and keeps the door open long enough for the homeowner to move his son into the garage; then the door shuts automatically, freeing the homeowner to stay with his son, rather than going back to shut the door. Another button in the garage triggers the same function for entering the home.

Convenient Features

The homeowners designed their kitchen to be chock-full of convenient features. Pull-out shelves in the base cabinets make it easy to access items stored at the back of the shelves. Tall pantry-style cabinets at one end of the kitchen eliminate the need for a separate pantry, allowing more square footage to be devoted to the kitchen. Other cabinets feature a built-in wastebasket and recycling bin, and cutlery dividers.

The desk area adjacent to the kitchen is "control central" for the family and keeps clutter off countertops and out of the kitchen. Upper cabinets in the desk area provide storage for cookbooks and binders; lower cabinets feature hanging file folders to keep family business in order and close at hand.

When planning a desk area near the kitchen, consider how you will use the space. Provide enough surface area for a phone, computer, and writing space, if necessary. Desk-area cabinets can be fitted with inserts suitable for books, files, computer hardware, and other specific storage functions. Under-cabinet lighting here, and throughout the kitchen, provides task lighting to illuminate desk work.

above One wall of the kitchen includes the stove, microwave, and refrigerator. Installing a microwave with venting capabilities above the stove saves valuable countertop space.

left Hanging-file inserts in the lower desk cabinets make it easy to keep family documents organized and off kitchen countertops.

above Pull-out shelves in all of the lower cabinets and in these pantry-style cabinets provide easy access to all stored items, expanding the amount of usable storage space available.

above Having a desk area adjacent to, but not part of, the kitchen is a great design strategy for keeping clutter out of the kitchen while making bill-paying and other record-keeping convenient.

above The opposite wall of this galley kitchen houses the dishwasher and sink, along with offering abundant storage and countertop space. Keeping plumbing fixtures along one wall minimizes the expense of the plumbing system.

above A sink with two bowls offers more flexibility, but it requires adequate counter space on both sides of the sink. The National Kitchen and Bathroom Association recommends at least 36 inches of open counter space on one side of a kitchen sink and at least 18 inches of open counter space on the other side.

Light and Bright

Because there are no windows within the main kitchen corridor, light color countertops and walls help make the kitchen bright and cheerful. The golden finish on the oak cabinets provides additional warmth to the room. Art tiles displayed above the sink offer a pleasant view while working at the sink. The pale floor tiles are kept bare. Area rugs might hamper wheelchair mobility.

above The desk area adjacent to the kitchen is "control central" for the family. There is plenty of room for a calendar and a hanging rack for house keys on the rear wall. Well-planned storage keeps the desktop clear for doing paperwork.

above The dining room is conveniently located just off one end of the kitchen. The same warm woods and neutral tones in the dining area connect it visually with the kitchen.

This contemporary kitchen provides ample space for food preparation and an inviting space for guests to linger while the homeowner is cooking.

Modern Gathering

This sleek, uncluttered open kitchen provides the ideal space for entertaining.

When this homeowner moved into his 1889 home, the house was crowded with tiny rooms that did not lend themselves to entertaining. With the goal of opening up the floor plan to develop a spacious environment worthy of a party, the homeowner envisioned how the small rooms could work together once certain walls were removed. The kitchen—now a sleek, open space—was a main component of the overall remodeling project. The kitchen is now an integral part of an open floor plan combined with an informal dining and conversation area. The formal dining room is accessible through an arched opening off the kitchen.

left Stainless steel and black appliances with a mix of white and silver-finish cabinets provide a visually pleasing combination of materials in the kitchen.

Material Choices

Smart choices about materials for your remodeling project can allow you to have the kitchen you desire within your budget. This homeowner originally considered granite or solid-surfacing countertops, but went with a more economical laminate to stay within his budget. He also delayed one aspect of the kitchen remodel—installing backsplashes—until he can have the granite backsplashes he desires.

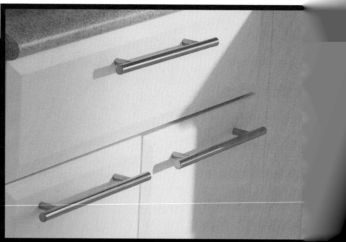

above right and right Stainless-steel door pulls create a strong horizontal line typical of contemporary design and make it easy to open doors and drawers. The pulls look streamlined against the silver-finish cabinets, and they pop against the white cabinets. The homeowner selected a gray-flecked laminate countertop because it is less expensive than granite or solid-surface and still coordinates with the overall look of the kitchen. The beveled curve of the countertop edge provides a clean look.

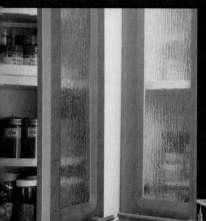

left Translucent glass panels on some of the cabinet doors create an interesting texture. Using translucent rather than transparent glass offers visual interest without the need to have display-ready items, because translucent glass somewhat distorts the shapes of the items.

left When the homeowner was in a home center design showroom, he saw cabinets with exposed legs and liked the look. After selecting standard cabinets for his kitchen, he removed the toe kicks and added legs fashioned from hardware sold in the plumbing and electrical department of the home center.

right This china hutch is actually three wall cabinets stacked on top of one another, creating a piece that is an extension of the kitchen's clean look.

right Laminate maple floors in a natural finish add to the light, clean look of the kitchen.

Contemporary Style

This kitchen with sleek, clean lines embodies much of the contemporary style noted for its uncluttered look and use of industrial materials. The homeowner selected cabinets in white and silver finishes. Though the cabinet doors have a slightly raised panel, the full-overlay style still provides the clean look consistent with this design style. Select cabinets feature glass panels with a translucent "rain" treatment. Horizontal lines—another element of contemporary design—are created by the long stainless-steel handles on the cabinet doors and drawers. The natural olive green wall color introduces a fresh, natural tone to the otherwise sleek, contemporary look of the kitchen. The metal and black sculptural chairs at the raised counter on the island offer seats for guests to visit with the homeowner as he prepares a meal, and they contribute to the modern appeal of this space. Leaving the window unadorned allows light to stream into the kitchen and affords great views. Likewise, the maple floor is kept free of area rugs that would visually clutter the room.

above Sleek pendent lights positioned near the cooktop island provide task and ambient light as well as a design element to the kitchen. Their slim profiles fit with the kitchen's decor.

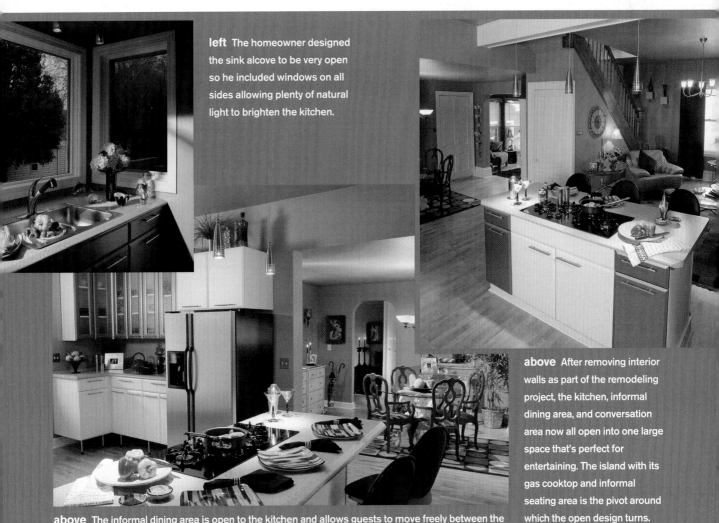

left The homeowner designed the sink alcove to be very open so he included windows on all sides allowing plenty of natural light to brighten the kitchen.

above After removing interior walls as part of the remodeling project, the kitchen, informal dining area, and conversation area now all open into one large space that's perfect for entertaining. The island with its gas cooktop and informal seating area is the pivot around which the open design turns.

above The informal dining area is open to the kitchen and allows guests to move freely between the two spaces. Using the same paint color in the informal dining area further visually connects the two areas into one large room.

CHAPTER 3

Planning

Making a workable and thorough plan to realize your new kitchen is probably the most important phase of a remodeling project. Without careful planning, the best design will fall short of expectations.

Now that you've learned a little about style and function, and spent some time with the ideas and examples in Chapter 2, you're ready to start planning your new kitchen. As you begin, the most important rules to remember are: ***do your homework*** and ***take your time***! Rushing decisions because of time pressures or impatience will make the process frustrating and exhausting. Following planning rules ensures you will create a kitchen that will give you years of pleasure and satisfaction.

CHAPTER 3 CONTENTS

left Putting in a new kitchen isn't easy; in fact, you need all the help you can get. Home centers provide a great support system for homeowners who are interested in a new kitchen. They offer design services, products, and even installation. Consulting professionals as you plan a new room will save you time and money, not to mention a few headaches along the way.

Getting Started

Planning your kitchen (and staying on budget) may seem a daunting task, but if you take a deep breath, do your homework, and go through the process one step at a time, before you know it, you will have achieved your goals.

Some Very Important Information

Many people have unpleasant experiences installing a new kitchen because they don't plan carefully and they don't give themselves enough time to complete the project. If you want a new kitchen in time for a holiday dinner, don't start demolition in late November. Construction is a business of surprises. No matter how thorough you are and how skilled and dedicated your contractor is, things will go wrong. Shipments could be delayed, parts could be damaged on delivery, there may be problems behind the walls, and the weather may not cooperate. The more room you have to compensate for the unexpected, the more successful and satisfying your experience will be.

Read This Chapter

Get an overview of the planning process by reading this chapter through (breeze through Chapter 4 as well) before you actually begin to put things on paper. A bit of general knowledge will help you sort out and make sense of what may seem to be a complicated and overwhelming process.

Get Specific

Start by charting your family's daily routine. Evaluate the features of your current kitchen, reflecting on what works well and what you hope to improve. Talk with other family members who will use the new kitchen. In your current arrangement, do people trip over one another trying to use the microwave oven and the stove at the same time each day? As the next step, consider how you see your kitchen being used: cooking, entertainment, reading, working, and snacking. Or maybe you prefer a no-frills utilitarian space. Are more windows, light, and a view a major priority?

Keep a Journal

For a week or so keep a journal to record how your kitchen is used, and describe any aggravations caused by the existing layout. Note times when it's too busy. List inconveniences in terms of storage and layout. Think of how you would use a stove top with a grill if you had one. Would two ovens make family holidays easier? Do other members of the family enjoy sharing cooking chores? For your own journal entries, start by thinking about your daily routine. Are there major traffic jams in the morning and evening, such as family members cutting through preparation and cooking centers? After every trip to the supermarket, do you rearrange the contents of your refrigerator so everything will fit? Do you face a similar puzzle when storing nonperishables? Are your cabinets boring? Does your garbage disposer make a racket against your stainless-steel sink? Do you back into the island when you open the oven door?

If you are in the kitchen much of the time, what do you enjoy? The view from the window sink? Would a skylight offer more natural light? Are all appliances still performing to satisfaction? Is your kitchen the neighborhood hangout—great for your children but getting a little too close for your comfort?

Fill Out the Checklists

The comprehensive checklists that follow in this chapter are meant to be useful tools throughout your planning process. You may find it helpful to make detailed notes about the elements in your current kitchen while developing your plan for the kitchen of your dreams. Prioritizing the features that are most important to you will be useful when the inevitable budget trade-offs become necessary. And remember to look to the future. A well-designed kitchen suits not only your current needs and circumstances but also accommodates lifestyle changes in the future.

No Mystery

This chapter takes the mystery out of two of the most critical parts of the planning process: developing a budget and sketching a detailed floor plan.

How It All Fits

Basic information on specifications and clearances for fixtures and products is included so you can have some idea of how the elements of your kitchen will all fit together as you devise a plan.

Making a Floor Plan

When you understand your needs and the basics of products and materials, you're ready to create a floor plan and start making some decisions about budget.

Developing a Budget

Getting the most kitchen for your money is only smart. Making a budget and sticking to it will relieve the inevitable stress that comes from preparing to invest a large amount of money in remodeling. Budgets not only set basic parameters, they help you track expenses and the progress of the job. The hardest part of any budget, of course, is sticking to it.

Great Advice

Equally important, you'll find great advice on determining the types of professionals you should hire, selecting professionals to interview, conducting interviews, hiring the building or design professional who is right for your job, entering into a contract for the project, and working with the professionals throughout the entire process. Finally don't be afraid to ask questions of the experts; experience is the best teacher.

sweet INSPIRATION

Whether you want to give your kitchen a facelift or build an addition, do not rush into making decisions. At this stage allow yourself to dream and gather ideas.

- Visit area show houses.
- Collect magazine pictures that depict room styles and elements that appeal to you.
- Talk with friends about their remodeling experiences.
- Surf the Internet for design ideas and product information.
- Collect product brochures and catalogs.
- Buy home repair books or check them out from the library. Learn the basics so you'll be prepared when it's time to consult professionals.
- Keep a small notebook in your purse or coat pocket to jot down great ideas or products.

Devise a record-keeping system. Use a ring binder with dividers and pockets. To get started turn to page 7, Chapter 1, and adapt the table of contents as a way to organize your binder. For example, you might have two major sections labeled Style and Function. In the Style section, you could label dividers for color schemes, decorating themes, and specific elements, such as sinks, surface materials, and accessories, that contribute to the look of your kitchen.

Use the Function section to track practical information about activity centers, layouts, general information about cabinet and counter space guidelines, appliances, ventilation, lighting, and electrical and plumbing requirements.

Make sure each divider has plenty of paper for the notes you'll take. At this stage don't hold back from recording your wildest notions.

Lifestyle Checklists

When assessing your current kitchen, take into account how you and your family use it daily, on weekends, and for special occasions, such as neighborhood get-togethers or formal entertaining. Think about what you like about the current space and what you would like to change. This checklist, which can be photocopied for your records, will come in handy when you map your dream kitchen later in this chapter.

YOU AND YOUR KITCHEN	YES	NO
Do you spend a lot of time in your kitchen on weekdays?	☐	☐
Do you spend a lot of time in your kitchen on the weekends?	☐	☐
Do you usually cook simple (heat-and-serve, one-dish, or crockery cooker) meals?	☐	☐
Do you regularly cook meals with several dishes?	☐	☐
Do you regularly cook and freeze make-ahead meals?	☐	☐
Do you enjoy cooking as a hobby?	☐	☐
If yes, do you cook gourmet meals?	☐	☐
If yes, do you can or freeze produce from the garden?	☐	☐
Other Kitchen Activities		
Working	☐	☐
Paying bills	☐	☐
Using a computer	☐	☐
Reading	☐	☐
Feeding pets	☐	☐
Recycling	☐	☐
Sorting or folding laundry	☐	☐
Gardening or potting	☐	☐
Making crafts	☐	☐
Sewing	☐	☐

YOUR FAMILY AND THE KITCHEN	YES	NO
Does your family have more than one cook?	☐	☐
Do your children or teenagers make snacks?	☐	☐
Do small children play in the kitchen?	☐	☐
Kitchen Uses		
Eating meals together	☐	☐
Relaxing and visiting	☐	☐
Watching television	☐	☐
Listening to music	☐	☐
Doing homework	☐	☐
Making crafts	☐	☐
Hanging out with friends after school	☐	☐
Casually entertaining friends and family	☐	☐
Formally entertaining	☐	☐

Kitchen Layout Checklists

Look at the work triangle and activity centers of your current kitchen in light of your lifestyle. Use this to note what you currently have and would like to have in your dream kitchen. (See pages 20–25 in Chapter 1 for information on access, the work triangle, and the food-preparation center.)

FOOD-PREPARATION CENTER	**YES**	**NO**
Sink Features		
Sufficient depth	☐	☐
Number of bowls		
Spout height, shape, and finish you desire		
Number and type of handles		
Soap dispenser	☐	☐
Spray with elongated handle	☐	☐
Hot-water dispenser	☐	☐
Do you have a secondary sink for washing and chopping produce?	☐	☐
Do you have a bar sink?	☐	☐
Do you have a garbage disposer?	☐	☐
Do you have a water filtration or purification system?	☐	☐
Do you have enough space for daily prep chores?	☐	☐
Do you have enough space for special activities, such as baking or cooking for many?	☐	☐
Do you have a lower section of countertop that kids can use for prep work?	☐	☐
Do you have adequate storage for:		
Frequently used canned and dry goods	☐	☐
Spices	☐	☐
Cooking utensils	☐	☐
Baking dishes, mixing bowls, and other cookware used during food prep	☐	☐
Mixers, blenders, and other small appliances	☐	☐
Everyday dishes	☐	☐
Special serving dishes, china, punch bowls, soup tureens, platters, trays, and silver	☐	☐
Flatware and serving utensils	☐	☐
Tablecloths and napkins	☐	☐
Do you desire more efficient food storage, such as lazy Susans and pull-out pantries?	☐	☐

EASY ACCESS	**YES**	**NO**
Are there entrances on both sides of the kitchen?	☐	☐
Doorways		
Open spaces	☐	☐
Pocket doors	☐	☐
Swinging doors	☐	☐
Do you have sufficient space for doorways?	☐	☐
Is there a convenient spot to hang up coats, remove dirty shoes, or set a heavy load?	☐	☐
Can people cut through the kitchen without disturbing the cook?	☐	☐
Do you find yourself taking many steps while cooking or cleaning up?	☐	☐
Are walkways wide enough?	☐	☐
Do you have sufficient room to maneuver:		
Between the sink and the refrigerator?	☐	☐
Between the sink and the cooktop/range?	☐	☐
To open the oven door?	☐	☐
If desired, do you have space for a work triangle for a second cook?	☐	☐

COOKING CENTER	YES	NO
Cooktop		
Electric	☐	☐
Gas	☐	☐
Smooth-top	☐	☐
Ventilation		
Overhead	☐	☐
Downdraft	☐	☐
Remote	☐	☐
Ranges		
Electric	☐	☐
Gas	☐	☐
Dual fuel	☐	☐
Warming drawers	☐	☐
Built-in grill	☐	☐
Ovens		
Electric	☐	☐
Gas	☐	☐
Do you want a new convection oven?	☐	☐
Do you want a new microwave oven?	☐	☐
Do you want a new microwave-convection oven?	☐	☐
Do you have quick, comfortable access to counters for hot pots?	☐	☐
Do you have enough counter space on both sides of the cooking surface?	☐	☐
Easy Access		
Pots, pans, and cooking utensils	☐	☐
Hot pads	☐	☐
Cooking oils, herbs, and seasonings	☐	☐
Cookbooks	☐	☐
New Small Appliances		
Blender	☐	☐
Deep fryer	☐	☐
Electric can opener	☐	☐
Crockery cooker	☐	☐
Knife sharpener	☐	☐
Electric wok	☐	☐
Food processor	☐	☐
Hand mixer	☐	☐
Meat grinder	☐	☐
Stand mixer	☐	☐
Toaster/Toaster oven	☐	☐
Bread machine	☐	☐
Coffee-, cappuccino-, espresso-maker	☐	☐
Ice cream/sorbet maker	☐	☐
Popcorn popper	☐	☐

DINING CENTER   YES   NO

Dining Style Preference (mark more than one if desired)

	YES	NO
Traditional dining table and chairs	☐	☐
Breakfast table and chairs	☐	☐
Island countertop with stools	☐	☐
Booth or banquette	☐	☐

	YES	NO
Is your eating area convenient to the hardworking areas of the kitchen?	☐	☐
Is there enough walkway behind diners?	☐	☐

Enough Space

	YES	NO
At the table	☐	☐
At the counter	☐	☐
At the island	☐	☐

CLEANUP CENTER   YES   NO

	YES	NO
Do you have enough cleanup space to stack dishes and unload the dishwasher?	☐	☐
Is your dishwasher located on a convenient side of the sink?	☐	☐
Do you have a trash container right at hand?	☐	☐
Do you have a nearby household recycling center?	☐	☐
Do you want a new dishwasher?	☐	☐
If yes, single unit?	☐	☐
If yes, dishwasher drawers?	☐	☐
Do you want a secondary dishwasher or a dishwasher drawer?	☐	☐

Extra Storage

	YES	NO
Dish towels	☐	☐
Dishrags	☐	☐
Sponges	☐	☐
Plastic bags	☐	☐
Cleaning products	☐	☐

SPECIALIZED CENTERS   YES   NO

Coffee or Beverage Center

	YES	NO
Second sink	☐	☐
Mini fridge	☐	☐
Separate icemaker	☐	☐
Wine cooler	☐	☐

Special Baking Center

	YES	NO
At least 36 inches of counter space	☐	☐
Extra cabinet space for special equipment	☐	☐
Do you desire a mini media center?	☐	☐

Space for Your Pets

	YES	NO
A feeding station	☐	☐
A place for a bed or crate	☐	☐

Laundry Area

	YES	NO
Stackable washer and dryer	☐	☐
Folding table	☐	☐
Pull-down or foldout ironing board	☐	☐

PLANNING AND COMMUNICATIONS CENTER

	YES	NO
Do you have a desk or mini office?	☐	☐
Is it located outside the work triangle?	☐	☐
Are your desk and chair comfortable?	☐	☐
Do you have a family message board, including calendars?	☐	☐
Do you want built-in cabinets and drawers?	☐	☐
Do you want an area for kids to do homework and store their supplies?	☐	☐

Desired Office Equipment

	YES	NO
Computer	☐	☐
Fax	☐	☐
Printer	☐	☐
Scanner	☐	☐
Do you need more space, outlets, and hookups for this equipment?	☐	☐

Basic Kitchen Layout

Now that you have given some thought to various kitchen centers, think about the layout that best suits your dream kitchen. Your current layout may work with modifications. Or you may need to open up space. Refer to basic kitchen layouts in Chapter 1. Which best describes the type of kitchen you are remodeling, renovating, or adding on?

BASIC KITCHEN LAYOUT

Single line (one-wall)	☐
Galley	☐
U-Shape	☐
U-Shape with island	☐
L-Shape	☐
Breaking out of L-Shape	☐
G-Shape (with or without island)	☐
Kitchen opening to great-room	☐
Kitchen opening to dining room	☐

Kitchen Appliances Checklists

Use these checklists to identify new and additional appliances you are considering for your new kitchen.

Note brands, models, and prices as you do your research.

OVENS, RANGES, AND COOKTOPS	**YES**	**NO**
Ranges — Types		
Conventional ovens/ranges (gas, electric, dual-fuel)	☐	☐
Built-in wall units	☐	☐
Freestanding	☐	☐
Drop in	☐	☐
Commercial style	☐	☐
Ranges — Features		
Self-cleaning	☐	☐
Continuous-clean	☐	☐
Control locks	☐	☐
Hot-surface indicator	☐	☐
Variable temperature broiling	☐	☐
Electronic controls	☐	☐
One-touch controls	☐	☐
Delay and time-bake cycles	☐	☐
Porcelain broiler pans	☐	☐
Separate warming drawer	☐	☐
Cooktops — Types		
Electrical-coil heat	☐	☐
Gas	☐	☐
Solid element	☐	☐
Sealed gas	☐	☐
Halogen	☐	☐
Induction	☐	☐
Dual-fuel	☐	☐
Indoor grills	☐	☐
Ice bin inside freezer door	☐	☐
Cooktops — Features		
Burner grates that can be removed easily for cleaning	☐	☐
Glass ceramic cooktops with radiant elements sealed beneath the surface	☐	☐
Flat-surface electronic control	☐	☐
Ovens — Types		
Gas	☐	☐
Electric	☐	☐
Single	☐	☐
Double	☐	☐
Thermal or radiant	☐	☐
Convection	☐	☐
Dual-fuel	☐	☐
Microwave — Types		
Built-in	☐	☐
Freestanding	☐	☐
Ventilation Hoods		
Updraft vent (ducted to the outside or filtered)	☐	☐
Downdraft vent	☐	☐
Remote	☐	☐

COLD STORAGE

	YES	NO
Refrigerators — Types		
Side-by-side	☐	☐
Freezer on top	☐	☐
Freezer on bottom	☐	☐
Built-in	☐	☐
Freestanding	☐	☐
Professional style	☐	☐
Refrigerators — Features		
Stainless-steel interior	☐	☐
Glass doors	☐	☐
Automatic defrost	☐	☐
Ice and water in door	☐	☐
Adjustable door bins	☐	☐
Adjustable tempered-glass shelves	☐	☐
Sliding shelves	☐	☐
Half-shelves that adjust to different heights	☐	☐
Shelves that fold away to fit large products	☐	☐
Spill guard	☐	☐
Window bins and see-through crisper drawers	☐	☐
Additional insulation	☐	☐
Separate temperature and moisture-level controls for meat and produce bins	☐	☐
Energy Star (means a model uses 10% less energy than standards allow)	☐	☐
Beverage capacity (door storage)	☐	☐
Top shelves that adjust with crank	☐	☐
Pull-out shelves/bins (some refrigerators have these in freezer and fridge)	☐	☐
Pull-out freezer wire baskets	☐	☐
See-through drawers	☐	☐
Child lockout	☐	☐
Speed icemaker	☐	☐
Wine cooler	☐	☐
Ice bin inside freezer door	☐	☐
Exterior Options		
Stainless steel	☐	☐
Color options	☐	☐
Trim panels to match cabinets	☐	☐
Other Cold Storage Options		
Separate upright freezer	☐	☐
Separate horizontal freezer	☐	☐
Refrigerator drawer	☐	☐
Under-counter snack refrigerator	☐	☐
Freezer drawer	☐	☐
Independent icemaker	☐	☐
Wine cooler	☐	☐

DISHWASHERS

	YES	NO
Dishwashers — Types		
Standard	☐	☐
Slide-in	☐	☐
Portable	☐	☐
Dishwasher Drawers		
Single	☐	☐
Stacked	☐	☐
Dishwasher — Features		
Sensors that adjust intensity of the wash cycle	☐	☐
Third rack	☐	☐
Upper rack	☐	☐
Water filters	☐	☐
Internal water heating	☐	☐
No-heat dry option	☐	☐
Built-in garbage disposers	☐	☐
Delayed starts	☐	☐
Pause function	☐	☐
Rinse-and-hold cycle	☐	☐
Pots-and-pans cycle	☐	☐
Well-insulated for noise reduction	☐	☐
Adjustable-height racks	☐	☐
Covered baskets and stemware holder	☐	☐
Multiple spray arms	☐	☐
Multiple settings and cycles	☐	☐
Interior Options		
Stainless steel	☐	☐
Plastic	☐	☐
Exterior Options		
Stainless steel	☐	☐
Hidden controls	☐	☐
Color options	☐	☐
Trim panels to match cabinets	☐	☐

Style and Materials Checklists

Decorating styles are not rigid as they were a generation ago. Now people feel free to use what appeals to them, tastefully combining influences without clashing. However, it's a good idea to decide on a general feel you want to achieve. Look through pictures and articles you have clipped. (See elements of style on pages 8–19 in Chapter 1 and kitchens featured in Chapter 2.) Which seem to characterize your personal style?

Materials Selection

Use the following checklists to identify the materials and other selections in your current kitchen and those you are considering for your new kitchen. Continue to consult your resources as you consider materials that suit your style. Look to specific elements in Chapter 4 for visual references. Remember to carefully match hardware to your doors and drawers.

CABINET MATERIALS	
Exterior Options	
Cherry	☐
White oak	☐
Red oak	☐
Birch	☐
Hickory	☐
Ash	☐
Pine	☐
Maple	☐
Laminate	☐
Polyester	☐
Stainless steel	☐
Door Styles	
Slab door (contemporary look)	☐
Frame and panel (raised panel)	☐
Frame and panel (arched panel)	☐
Frame and panel (beaded)	☐
Recessed panel (Shaker)	☐
Frame and flat panel	☐
Doors with glass panes (clear for display)	☐
Doors with glass panes (with textured glass)	☐

COUNTERTOPS AND BACKSPLASH	
Laminate (prefab or special order)	☐
Ceramic tile (stock or custom, such as hand-painted)	☐
Solid-surfacing	☐
Solid-surface veneer	☐
Stone tile and slabs (marble, limestone, slate, soapstone, lavastone, sandstone, granite, or marble tiles)	☐
Cultured marble	☐
Butcher block or hardwood	☐
Stainless steel	☐
Copper	☐
Cast concrete	☐
Engineered stone (quartz combined with resins and pigments)	☐
Glass and mirror (also used in backsplash)	☐

Flooring

If you are considering a change in your flooring, ask yourself these questions. What material is used in your current flooring? Does your current flooring stand up well to foot traffic and the occasional spill and moisture? Do you plan to replace the flooring? What type of flooring is used in adjacent rooms? Which seems to be the better choice?

FLOORING	
Laminate	☐
Stone tile (marble, limestone, slate, granite)	☐
Ceramic tile	☐
Concrete	☐
Wood	☐
Resilient	☐
Stainless steel	☐
Copper	☐
Skid resistant (examples: textured tile and vinyl)	☐
Carpet	☐
Other	☐

General Guidelines

It is helpful to review general specifications and guidelines for minimum clearance recommendations and fixture placement, which are recommended by the National Kitchen and Bath Association (NKBA) and other experts. Refer to this information later in this chapter when you are creating your floor plan. Using this information will help you analyze the available space, consider all of the recommended clearance guidelines, and see whether your dream will fit. If not, it's back to the drawing board for another try.

Remember that these are only guidelines. Some rules may not apply to your layout or particular needs. Your kitchen may work better if your available area allows you to include storage space and elbowroom beyond those recommended by the guidelines.

Cabinet Guidelines

Having enough room to store food, dishes, utensils, pots, pans, appliances, and other items is a challenge, especially when you accumulate stuff over time. Of course it's wise to clear out unused items. Remember, every square inch is precious.

For smaller kitchens less than 150 square feet, plan for:

- At least 156 inches of base cabinet frontage. (Calculate by combining the widths of all base cabinets. When calculating the minimums, count only base cabinets that are at least 21 inches deep, but note that the blind portion of a blind corner cabinet does not count.)
- At least 144 inches of wall cabinet frontage. (When calculating the minimums, count only wall cabinets that are at least 30 inches high and 12 inches deep and that have adjustable shelving. Also note that difficult-to-reach cabinets above the range hood, oven, or refrigerator should not be included in the total unless they are outfitted with devices to improve accessibility.)
- At least 120 inches of drawer or roll-out shelf frontage. (This is calculated by multiplying the number of drawers by the width of the units; for example, a 24-inch-wide unit with three drawers would provide 72 inches of space to count toward the recommended 120-inch minimum total. When calculating the minimums, include only those drawers that are at least 15 inches wide and 21 inches deep.)

avoid the
RAZOR'S EDGE

Eliminate sharp corners on countertops by requesting models with rounded or clipped corners and eased edges.

For kitchens larger than 150 square feet, plan for:

- At least 192 inches of base cabinet frontage. (Combine the widths of all cabinets; when calculating the minimums, count only base cabinets that are at least 21 inches deep, and note that the blind portion of a blind corner cabinet does not count.)
- At least 186 inches of wall cabinet frontage. (When calculating the minimums, count only wall cabinets that are at least 30 inches high and 12 inches deep and have adjustable shelving. Also note that difficult-to-reach cabinets above the range hood, oven, or refrigerator should not be included in the total unless they are outfitted with devices to improve accessibility.)

- At least 165 inches of drawer or roll-out shelf frontage. (This is calculated by multiplying the number of drawers by the width of the units; for example, a 24-inch-wide unit with three drawers would provide 72 inches of space to count toward the recommended 165-inch minimum. Drawers or roll-out shelves must be at least 15 inches wide and 21 inches deep to count.)

For any size kitchen:

- Plan for at least 60 inches of wall cabinet frontage by the sink, located within 72 inches of the primary sink centerline. These cabinets should be at least 12 inches deep and at least 30 inches high. Note: A tall cabinet can be substituted for the recommended wall cabinets if it is placed within 72 inches of the sink centerline.
- When calculating the width of cabinets, diagonal or pie-cut wall cabinets should usually be counted as providing a total of 24 inches.
- When calculating the width of cabinets, pie-cut or lazy Susan base cabinets should usually be counted as providing a total of 30 inches.
- To improve functionality and accessibility, plan for at least five storage or organizing items in the kitchen. These items should be located between 15 and 48 inches above the floor (or extending into that area). Examples include bins or racks, swing-out pantries, interior vertical dividers, lowered wall cabinets, raised base cabinets, tall cabinets, appliance garages, and specialized drawers and shelves. Full-extension drawers and roll-out shelves (if they are in addition to those counted to reach the 120-inch minimum for small kitchens or 165-inch minimum for larger kitchens) may also be included.
- Use those corners: If your kitchen has usable corner areas, it is recommended to include at least one functional corner storage unit.
- Are tall cabinets counted as wall or base units? Cabinets that are 72 inches or taller can count as either base cabinets or wall cabinets, but not both. The calculation for various depth tall units is as follows:
  - 12-inch-deep tall units = 1 × the base lineal footage, 2 × the wall lineal footage.
  - 18-inch-deep tall units = 1.5 × the base lineal footage, 3 × the wall lineal footage.
  - 21- to 24-inch-deep tall units = 2 × the base lineal footage, 4 × the wall lineal footage.

Base Cabinets

The typical base cabinet—a single drawer over a door—can vary in width from 12 to 24 inches. In the sink-base version, the width is typically 30 inches and the drawer is usually false. The sink usually takes up the space needed for a drawer, so the drawer in a sink base is usually just a drawer front screwed to the cabinet.

Drawer bases have two to four drawers that are from 12 to 36 inches wide.

Base cabinets with double doors and single shelves range from 27 to 48 inches wide.

Wall Cabinets

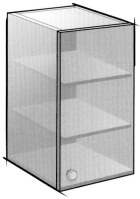

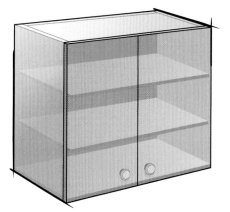

Single-door wall cabinets range in width from 9 to 24 inches. Standard 30-inch-high cabinets have two adjustable shelves. Also available in heights ranging from 36 to 42 inches.

Double-door wall cabinets range in width from 24 to 48 inches. Units without a center stile, like this one, will give you better access to the shelves. Heights range from 12 to 42 inches.

Corner and Sink-Base Cabinets

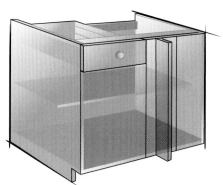

Double-door sink-base cabinets range from 24 to 48 inches wide and can double as built-in range bases. They can have one or two false-drawer fronts. Some models have working drawers at the bottom or stain- and moisture-resistant tilt-out trays on the top.

Blind-corner base cabinets join two runs of cabinets at right angles. To make the adjoining cabinet line up with it, the end of the cabinet may need to be positioned a few inches from the wall, making it occupy a little more wall space than its actual width (36 to 48 inches).

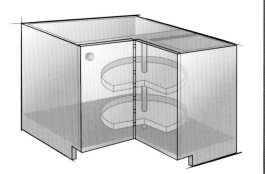

A corner cabinet with a lazy Susan occupies 33 to 36 inches of wall on each side of the corner. It takes best advantage of corner storage space. These units have bifold doors.

abbreviations: **TALK THE TALK**

If you look through a catalog on kitchen cabinets, you'll find all sorts of codes used to describe the cabinets. Usually they're something like WC2436, which translates like this:

■ The first character denotes the general type: W = wall; T = tall; B = base; V = vanity; D = desk.

■ The second set of characters refers to the specific type of cabinet: BB = blind base; BC = blind corner; BD = base with drawers; C = corner.

■ The next two are the height in inches.

■ The next two digits are the unit's width in inches.

■ Any other designations for special features such as glass doors are vendor specific.

Corner and Specialty Cabinets

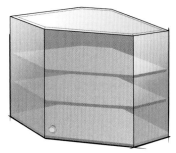

Surface that adjoining unit butts against

Diagonal corner cabinets, although more costly than blind corner units, make best use of storage space. Most occupy 24 inches of wall on each side of the corner and have two shelves.

Blind corner wall cabinets join two runs of cabinets at right angles. To make the adjoining cabinet line up with it, the end of a cabinet may need to be positioned a few inches from the wall, making it occupy a little more wall space than its actual width (24 to 48 inches). Most of the corner remains available for storage, but the deepest reaches of the cabinet are hard to access.

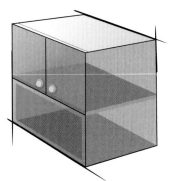

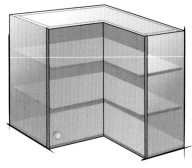

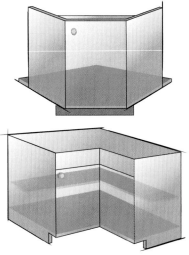

Wall cabinets holding microwave ovens are usually 30 to 32 inches wide, 36, 40, or 42 inches high, and 12, 15, 18, or 21 inches deep. Units designed for built-in front-vented ovens are 18 inches deep. Additional support either underneath or on both sides is required.

Most pie-cut corner cabinets call for 24 inches of wall on each side of the corner. The bifold door (curved doors are also available) solves clearance problems. They come in heights of 30, 36, and 42 inches.

Both a diagonal sink-base unit *(top)* or a 90° corner sink-base cabinet *(above)* occupy from 36 to 42 inches of wall space on each side of the corner. Bifold doors provide best access to storage. They also require a custom countertop with a diagonal that matches the one on the cabinet.

Wall-oven cabinets are 24 to 33 inches wide and 84 to 96 inches high. Some have storage both above and below the oven section.

Utility cabinets come in all sorts of shapes and sizes. They can be from 84 to 96 inches tall, 12 to 36 inches wide, and 12 to 24 inches deep. Most have four or five adjustable or sliding shelves.

Countertop Guidelines

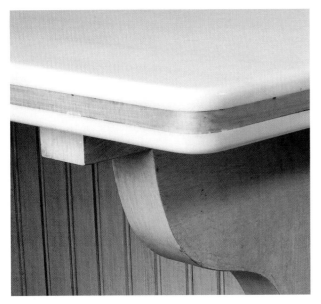

Usable countertop frontage recommendations:
- For small kitchens allow at least 132 inches of usable countertop length.
- For larger kitchens allow at least 198 inches of usable countertop length.

Basic measurements:
- Counters should be at least 16 inches deep.
- Wall cabinets should be at least 15 inches above the countertop surface for that area to be included when calculating the total usable countertop frontage.
- Corner space should not be counted.
- If a cabinet or an appliance garage extends to the counter, there must be 16 inches of clear space in front of this cabinet for the area to be included when calculating the total usable countertop frontage.

By the Sink
- For primary sinks, have at least 24 inches of countertop length on one side of the primary sink and at least 18 inches on the other side. (The 24-inch countertop frontage should be at the same counter height as the sink.)
- When calculating countertop frontage, the total of two-angled countertop sections can be counted, but only the countertop frontage should be measured; that is, do not count corner space.
- If the primary sink is near a corner, the edge of the primary sink should be at least 3 inches from the corner; the recommendation is to leave at least 15 inches from that corner to the sink centerline.

- If there is less than 18 inches of countertop frontage from the edge of the primary sink to a corner, then it is recommended to allow 21 inches of clear counter on the return.
- For secondary sinks have at least 3 inches of countertop length on one side and 18 inches on the other. (The 18-inch countertop frontage should be at the same counter height as the sink.)

Smooth Landing in The Cooking Area
Allow for at least 15 inches of landing space by the microwave oven, a minimum of 16 inches deep, above, below, or beside. By the cooktop, allow for at least 9 inches of counter space on one side of the cooking surface and 15 inches on the other. This allows the cook to turn handles away from the front of the cooktop and provides a place for setting hot pots coming directly off the cooktop. The landing space on both sides should be at the same counter height as the appliance. If your cooking surface is located by an end wall, allow for at least 3 inches of clearance space at the end wall (which should be protected by flame-retardant surfacing material) and 15 inches on the other side of the appliance. Again the landing space on both sides should be at the same counter height as the appliance. If there is no abutting wall or backsplash, the countertop should extend a minimum of 9 inches behind the cooking surface at the same counter height as the appliance.

By the Refrigerator
On the handle side of the refrigerator, allow for at least 15 inches of counter space (plan for 15 inches on both sides if your refrigerator is a side-by-side model). This recommended 15-inch minimum of landing space can be on a countertop across from the refrigerator as long as it is no more than 48 inches away.

By the Oven
Allow for at least 15 inches of countertop landing space next to the oven. This counter space should be at least 16 inches deep. The landing space can be a countertop across from the oven at no more than 48 inches away as long as the oven door does not open into a traffic area.

Preparation Centers
- Plan for at least 36 inches of uninterrupted countertop space for the food-preparation center.
- This counter space should be at least 16 inches deep.

Appliance Guidelines

Floor Space and Clearance

At the sink, dishwasher, cooktop, oven, and refrigerator, provide a clear floor space of 30×48 inches. (Measure from the face of a cabinet or appliance if the toe-kick is less than 9 inches high.) The minimum suggested floor spaces can overlap. Up to 19 inches of knee space (beneath an appliance, counter, cabinet, or other structure) may be included as part of the total 30-inch or 48-inch dimension.

Microwave Ovens

- The recommendation is to place a microwave oven so that the bottom of the appliance is 24 to 48 inches above the floor.
- A different placement height may be desired, depending on the principal user's physical abilities.

By the Cooktop

- For safety provide at least 30 inches of clearance between a cooktop and the bottom of an unprotected surface (such as a wood cabinet located above the cooktop).
- If the surface above is a protected surface, the clearance recommendation can be reduced to 24 inches.
- If the protected surface is a microwave oven-ventilation hood combination, check the manufacturer's specifications for recommended clearance.
- Do not place the cooktop under a window unless the window is 3 inches or more behind the appliance, and more than 24 inches above it. Remember that flammable window treatments should never be used on windows above a cooking surface.

At the Dishwasher

- Allow for a minimum of 21 inches of clear floor space between the edge of the dishwasher and counters, appliances, and/or cabinets, that are placed at a right angle to the dishwasher.
- The edge of the dishwasher should be within 36 inches of the edge of the sink.
- Make the dishwasher accessible to more than one person at a time. This will accommodate other cooks and those on cleanup duty.

above Look for dishwashers with well-designed interiors that maximize space for dishes and that protect delicate glassware. Stainless steel provides a highly durable shell.

Ventilation Guidelines

Proper ventilation eliminates lingering odors in the kitchen and throughout the house. It also stops grease from slowly covering surfaces in your kitchen and prevents moisture from loosening wallpaper and generating mold and mildew. The ventilation system you choose should have a fan rated at a minimum of 150 cfms (cubic feet per minute). There are many choices, including traditional over-the-cooktop range hoods, hidden models for over the cooktop, and various types of downdraft models.

An updraft vent, or over-the-cooktop range hood, can be a major focal point. The design possibilities, materials, and color choices are almost endless.

Vent Hoods

Vent hoods are generally the most efficient and effective at removing moisture, grease, and odors from the kitchen. As cooking vapors rise, they inhale steam and smoke. These models can be ducted to the outside, double vented, remote vented, or merely filtered. A ducted hood ventilates more thoroughly. With nonducted models, the internal filter will need to be replaced or cleaned on a regular basis.

Downdraft

A downdraft model ventilation system, which must be ducted to the outside, is a good choice for island cooking or any other spot that isn't conducive to a large overhead hood. The low profile offered by a downdraft model is appealing to some homeowners. Standard downdraft vents look like an extra section of grill built into a cooktop. Another option is a pop-up model, which remains below the counter until needed.

Built-Ins

Another option is a panel design type of range hood that is installed under or built into a wall-mounted microwave oven or on the bottom of a wall cabinet. These models are streamlined and hidden from view when not in use. They do not perform as well as traditional vent hoods, but remain a popular option where there is limited space or for those who do little frying or other high-heat cooking.

right Vent hoods that are ducted to the outside remove odors and grease most efficiently. Vent hoods can be the focus of a kitchen or they can slide out when being used as shown here.

VENTILATION basics

- Both updraft vent hoods and downdraft models use a fan or blower to pull moisture, cooking fumes, and heat out of the house through a system of ducts. Some ovens are remote- or double-vented.
- Include the ductwork in your kitchen layout during the planning process. If you choose a downdraft system, the ducts are often installed beneath the floor or inside cabinet toe-kicks. If you have existing ductwork, ensure it is the appropriate size for your new system.
- If you have a standard cooktop, the updraft vent or range hood should extend 3 inches past the sides of the cooktop. With larger, commercial-style cooktops add approximately 6 more inches on each side.
- The manufacturer usually recommends installing a range hood 24 to 30 inches above the cooktop. Smaller range hoods need to be close to the cooktop.
- The performance of a ventilation system is rated according to how many cfms (cubic feet per minute) of air it moves.
- Noise level is rated in sones. The sound generated by a ventilation system is a combination of the fan, the motor, and the movement of air through the duct system.
- Higher performing systems make more noise, creating a trade-off between noise level and quality of performance.
- When choosing a model consider that a larger motor with a variable-speed switch running at less than full speed will be quieter than a smaller motor running at maximum capacity.
- Other tips for reducing noise are to mount the motor away from the kitchen near the external vent and to plan for ductwork with as few turns as possible on the way to the outside.

Lighting Guidelines

A winning kitchen design has the right combination of artificial lighting and natural light. Adequate lighting adds to the beauty, efficiency, and safety of your space. With artificial lighting, you need to plan for the best mix of ambient, task, and accent lighting.

Accent Lighting

Accent lights used to highlight collectibles showcased inside a cabinet, artwork, or an interesting architectural feature, can increase the design impact of your kitchen area. These lights are typically about three times more powerful than general lighting. Low-voltage halogen bulbs are a good choice, as is a recess downlight with an eyeball lens pointing a beam of light in a particular direction.

Ambient Lighting

Ambient lighting is soft general lighting that spans the room. During the day sunlight can provide much of the kitchen's ambient lighting. You also should install adequate ceiling fixtures, track lighting, and/or recessed fixtures. Lighting from ceiling fixtures alone can create unpleasant shadows. To fix this locate bulbs on cabinet tops and aim them to reflect off the ceiling. This adds soft, sculpted light to the environment. This approach is recommended only for walls with no-gloss paint to avoid harsh reflections.

How much light is enough? With ambient lighting you should plan to have at least 100 watts of incandescent light or 75 watts of fluorescent light for each 50 square feet of floor space. You need to consider the height of your ceiling and the color of your walls. Darker colors tend to absorb light, so if your decorating scheme relies on darker tones, you may need to plan for additional lighting.

Task Lighting

Task lighting provides a direct beam of light to areas above sinks and to food preparation and cleanup centers. Install the task fixtures in front of where you will be working to avoid shadows.

Many types of fixtures, including recessed downlights, track lights, hanging pendent lights, and undercabinet strip lights, provide excellent task lighting. It's best to have the lighting for each work center controlled by its own separate wall switch.

How much task lighting do you need? Each work center should be illuminated with either 100 to 150 watts of incandescent light or 40 to 50 watts of fluorescent light. What about undercabinet lighting? To light countertops that have cabinets overhead, strip lighting is needed. These fixtures have a thin profile and are almost hidden. As a general rule a fluorescent tube should extend along approximately two-thirds of the counter it is illuminating and provide about 8 watts of power per foot of counter space.

Every work surface in the kitchen should be well illuminated by task or general lighting.

Natural Lighting

Maximizing the available natural light is a critical element in most kitchen design plans. Consider adding windows or French doors or perhaps a skylight. If you are the primary cook and spend many hours preparing meals, you might enjoy a large, cheery window above the sink. Windows also provide fresh air, which helps eliminate heat and odors from the kitchen and surrounding areas.

There are ways to increase natural lighting even if you don't have additional wall space to dedicate to windows. Consider replacing existing windows with taller units or add an additional fixed, arch-top window over an existing window.

Remember, though, that additional light can also mean unwelcome heat during the summer, so be sure to plan for a way to shade the windows during that time of year.

Flooring Guidelines

Choose flooring materials that are appropriate for how the room will be used. Kitchens should be covered in durable materials such as hardwoods, nonslippery tile, natural stone, vinyl, or laminate. Indoor/outdoor carpeting can be used in dry climates where conditions permit. For information on flooring options see the Shopping Guide in Chapter Four, page 147.

Safety First

Safety is a primary concern when choosing kitchen flooring. Falls are dangerous for everyone but especially so for the elderly, children, and those who are physically challenged. The majority of slips and falls that occur inside households are caused by improper installation and maintenance of materials, a buildup of grease and grime, extensive wear, and the properties of the flooring material itself. You can avoid many accidents if you put the right flooring materials in the right places and properly maintain them. Some potentially slippery situations in kitchens follow.

- Hard surfaces, which are often naturally slippery, especially when highly polished or naturally glossy.
- Grease spills or sticky spots left unattended or water puddled on a kitchen floor.
- Loose tiles or floorboards, as well as protruding nails or staples.
- Uneven transitions between rooms or types of flooring.
- Flooring material that visually obscures transitions between levels.
- Wooden floors that are not properly sanded and sealed. (They present the risk of splinters for bare feet.)

Least Slippery Flooring

The least slippery surfaces are rubber, textured surfaces, low-pile or indoor/outdoor carpet, surfaces with low-gloss or no-gloss finishes, and surfaces that absorb water. Even the safest surfaces must be properly installed, consistently cleaned, and well-maintained to ensure against accidents.

Cleaning and Maintenance

Any flooring material will need cleaning and maintenance on a regular basis. Regular care lengthens the life of your floor, guarantees that warranties will be honored, and keeps the surface looking its best. Once the floor is in use, dirt, stains, scratches, and tears are inevitable. The longer the time between cleanings and repair, the worse the problem becomes.

How much are you willing to do? The amount of care a floor needs after installation and the amount of time you are willing to spend taking care of it are crucial design and planning considerations.

above and below Maintenance requirements vary even among similar materials. Ceramic tile requires less maintenance than natural stone, which must be resealed and polished occasionally. Hardwoods also require reapplication of sealers and finishes as they wear.

structural CONCERNS

New floors? Heavy appliances? Taking down walls? If you are replacing the floor, consider the weight of the new material you have selected and find out whether the floor structure can support the new flooring. Be careful with load-bearing walls; always consult a professional.

Decide how much time you want to spend on care and maintenance. Pick your flooring to fit your lifestyle. While all flooring must be properly maintained, more exotic materials such as cork require more care.

Plumbing Guidelines

Considerations

- Will you be moving the sink and/or adding a second sink? If yes, water pipes and drains will have to be moved and expenses will increase.

- Are you considering adding a water filtration system or a hookup for an icemaker and water filter in the refrigerator?
- Make sure that all plumbing meets local code for both the supply and drain sides.
- Local codes dictate that sinks must be situated a specific distance from side walls and must have a certain amount of clear floor space in front of them.
- Remember that pipes in exterior walls need to be well insulated.
- Do you have pipes that should be replaced? While the walls are already down is the time to do it!
- Keep in mind that if a sink is installed in a load-bearing wall, the structural integrity of the framing will have to be maintained.
- No joists should be cut in the floor to route pipes to the vertical stack. This is to maintain the structural integrity of the floor.
- If you don't feel comfortable doing the plumbing yourself, hire a professional.

Electrical Guidelines

The Basics

Most kitchens will require at least seven separate circuits. The major appliances (except for the refrigerator) each need their own dedicated circuits.

- Range: Separate 240-volt circuit.
- Dishwasher: Separate 120-volt circuit.
- Microwave oven: Separate 120-volt circuit.
- Kitchen lighting: Requires one general lighting circuit.
- Garbage disposer: Separate 120-volt circuit.
- Smaller appliances: At least two additional 120-volt, 20-amp ground fault circuit interrupter (GFCI) countertop receptacles spaced no more than 4 feet apart, so that no part of your countertop is more than 24 inches from a power source.

- Also consider: telephone jacks, separate computer lines, Internet, and coaxial television cable.
- Extra wiring for lighting under cabinets and soffits.
- New circuits may need a larger electrical panel. Installing a new panel should be done by a licensed electrician.
- Determine the wattage of your appliances. Add up the wattage of those appliances you plan to plug into each circuit. Below are common wattage ratings for small appliances you may have:

Microwave oven	500–1,200 watts
Blender	200–500 watts
Toaster	800–1,200 watts
Toaster oven	1,500 watts
Coffeemaker	600–1,000 watts
Food processor	300–500 watts

- GFCI protection should be specified on all receptacles in the kitchen that are near water sources. GFCI receptacles are also required above all countertops.
- Wall-mounted controls should be positioned no higher than 48 inches above the finished floor. This includes light switches, thermostats, wall receptacles, telephones, and intercoms.

Creating a Floor Plan

frequently asked
LAYOUT
QUESTIONS

Can somebody else do the drawings?

Drawings can be prepared by designers at home centers and by architects and designers, but it's helpful to map the space and have some ideas before you meet with a pro. Better preparation means more productive work sessions.

What if I'm doing it all myself?

If you will be actively involved in the construction phase, then your drawings are much more critical and must be very accurate. Numerous online tools are available. Have your drawings checked by professionals, and comply with all local codes.

What if I'm not moving appliances?

With many kitchen remodeling and renovation projects, the homeowners choose to leave the refrigerator, sink, and dishwasher where they are, a decision that greatly reduces the cost. If that is your plan, you probably don't need to go to all the trouble of drawing floor plans and elevation views but you will still need to measure and consult with a professional.

What's the difference between a floor plan and an elevation?

A floor plan is an overhead view of the entire space on one piece of paper. This is the view that best shows the layout and traffic patterns, window and door placement, and locations of appliances and cabinetry and fixed objects. An elevation view is drawn from the perspective of one looking directly at an interior wall. It indicates scale and proportions, but it is a two-dimensional drawing and will not show perspective. Separate elevation drawings of each wall are required. Studying the elevation views can also uncover potential clearance problems.

What tools do I need to get started?

Two tape measures (one preferably 50 feet long) and a stepladder. You also need ¼-inch graph paper, tracing paper, a notepad, pencils, a scale (architect's) ruler, and erasers. Recruit a helper for measuring; the results will be far more accurate.

Starting the Layout Process

A kitchen remodel offers more flexibility in terms of moving the position of major features because, unlike a bathroom where repositioning the toilet or shower can lead to major changes in waste and drain lines, new routes for plumbing and electricity are easier to accomplish. But even if you're not changing the basic work triangle, an accurate floor plan is still essential. There are three options for developing a layout. You can do the layout by hand, hire an architect, or take advantage of a computer design program.

No matter what method you use to develop a layout, you must still measure the room accurately and at least create a rough sketch of the space.

The National Kitchen and Bath Association (NKBA) has developed guidelines that help create the safest and most comfortable kitchens, and your installation must meet national and local building codes. When you plan your kitchen, meet as many guidelines as you can—but even the NKBA says it can be difficult to meet them all. We've grouped them into five sidebars and present them as they come up in the process so they can be easily followed. Once you're done, take your plans to a designer and then to a building inspector for input.

How to Measure

Most experts recommend that you draw your floor plan in two stages; begin with a rough sketch and later refine it, making it a more precise scale drawing of your space.

Draw a **rough outline** of your kitchen on graph paper, marking off windows, doors, appliances, and other fixed elements. If you would like to enlarge the area, note any adjacent space that you might consider for expansion.

■ Start at the corners and measure the length and width of the kitchen. It's OK to round off the dimensions and measurements to the nearest ½ inch. (For the final drawings it is better to be more precise and round down to the nearest ⅛ inch.)

■ The next step is to measure the spaces between all the elements you have noted. Be sure to record all the measurements on your drawing as you proceed. It's best to measure in inches (rather than feet and inches).

■ Check to see if the individually recorded measurements/distances along each wall add up to the total length you had recorded. Also make sure the total measurement of opposite walls is equal. If not, check your work.

■ Draw an elevation view of each wall in the kitchen. To do this measure the height of the ceilings, doors, windows, cabinets, appliances, and other such elements. If there is a vaulted ceiling or varying ceiling heights, note this.

Drafting to Scale

To prepare detailed drawings you need to decide on the scale (inches to feet on the drawing) that will properly represent the details you need. For larger kitchens start with a scale of ½ inch on paper equals 1 foot in the room. For smaller kitchens you might want to start with a scale of 1 inch on paper equals 1 foot in the room.

To double-check for accuracy, remeasure the outside dimensions of the room, the openings, doors and windows, interior wall thicknesses (measured at the doorways), and all other fixed elements. Mark the location and dimensions of outlets and switches, pipes (hot and cold water lines and drainage lines), gas lines, and vent ducts. For outlets, for example, measure the distance from the left-hand corner of the wall where the outlet is located to the center of the cover plate. Also measure the distance between the center of the cover plate and the floor.

Floor Plan by Hand

Following is the order of work for laying out a kitchen floor plan by hand. It requires only a tape measure, pencil, ruler, and graph paper.

■ Start by measuring the space. Then draw an overhead floor plan of the room and add your measurements.

■ Place the fixtures—refrigerator, sink, dishwasher, range, and cooktop—one by one. As you add each element, subtract the wall space it occupies from the amount available to make sure everything will fit.

Create a Final Floor Plan

One easy way to use this base floor-plan drawing is to make several photocopies, then experiment with different layouts and configurations. Another popular approach is to use tracing paper. You can trace the walls with changes you are considering, then try various ways to fit the sink, stove, refrigerator, and cabinetry in new locations. Since you're not writing on the actual floor plan, you can do this as many times as you wish. Refer to the NKBA and other space guidelines on the following pages while you work through various options. And remember the details, such as space needed for doors and drawers. Using cutouts that represent cabinets and fixtures that can be moved around the floor plan may be helpful as long as they're cut accurately to scale.

For a more detailed look at how to draft a final floor plan see pages 100–105.

Floor Plan by Computer

Computer design programs have replaced most of the hard work involved in laying out a kitchen. Most home centers have computers available that will create floor plans and elevations from dimensions you provide, or they will measure the space for you. There are also many software options available commercially, but not all are compatible with every computer.

The program will develop plans and build a three-dimensional rendering so you can take a virtual tour of the space.

A Sample Kitchen Floor Plan

Even in this age of standardization, no two kitchens are quite the same dimensions, but basic principles of layout and design will guide you through the process and allow you to fit everything properly into the space. The sample layout that unfolds on the following pages is based on an average-sized U-shape kitchen. NKBA guidelines are included along the way to help you make decisions about functionality and safety.

Use the Subtraction Method

In the subtraction method, you first create the work triangle and then fill the rest of the space with cabinets, counters, and accessories. As you add each element, subtract the wall space it occupies from the amount available until, with the last piece, you've filled all the space.

When you plan your kitchen, try to meet as many guidelines as possible but keep in mind that it may be tough meeting them all.

❶ Place the Sink Base Cabinet

In this example Wall 1 is 97 inches long, Wall 2 is 144 inches long, and Wall 3 is 87 inches long. The window, including the trim, is 42 inches wide. It's 45 inches from Wall 1 and 57 inches from Wall 3.

The sink could face the family room. It could be in a corner. Here it's centered at a window. Draw a line through the center of the window. The kitchen has a 36-inch-wide double-bowl sink base; each edge is 18 inches from the center of the window. Count over the right number of

squares and draw in the edges of the sink. Sketch in the front of the sink 24 inches from Wall 2. Make sure that the sink will have between 24 to 36 inches of counter space on one side, and 18 to 36 inches on the other. If you're right-handed, give the right side of the sink the extra space.

Remember, the sink does not have to be centered on the wall. Placing it off center often will provide more functional space with fewer fillers and more storage.

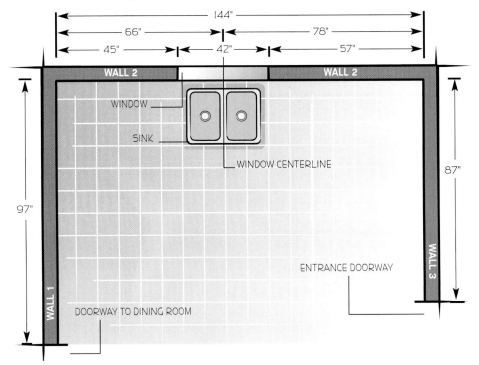

❷ Lay Out the Work Triangle

Place the range and refrigerator in position with the sink to form an efficient work triangle. In a U-shape kitchen, put the range on one wall adjoining the sink wall and put the refrigerator on the other. Pick locations that are most practical. Here are things to think about:

■ Position the range so you can get to the table easily.

■ Provide at least 9 inches of counter space on one side of the range and 15 inches on the other side.

■ Never locate a range under a window.

■ Place the refrigerator at the end of a cabinet run.

■ Make sure the refrigerator will have 18 inches of counter space on the handle side.

■ Make sure the refrigerator door can swing open completely and away from the work triangle, but not into a doorway. (Some models offer reversible hinges.)

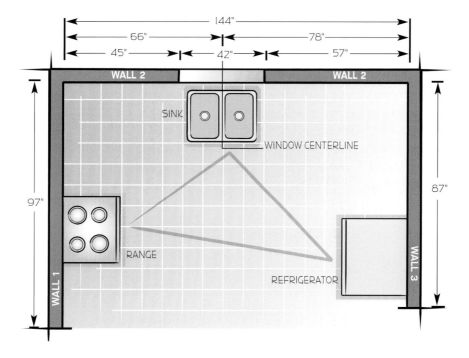

❸ Draw In the Basic Outline of the Cabinets

Even if you don't yet know which style cabinets you're going to choose, you may know that the base cabinets are going to be 24 inches deep and the wall cabinets are going to be 12 inches deep. Draw dotted lines on your sketch, according to the right number of squares from the walls, to indicate the depth of the wall and base cabinets.

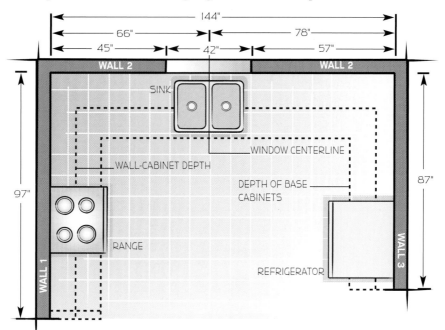

❹ Choose the Base Cabinets Along the Sink Wall

Start at the centerline of the window and work to the right. A double-bowl sink requires a 36-inch-wide sink base unit. Measure to the right half its width (18 inches) from the center of the window. That leaves 60 inches to the right of the window (78 inches–18 inches). The dishwasher (24 inches wide) goes to the right of the sink base. That leaves 36 inches in the right-hand corner.

Now work to the left of the window. Measuring from the window center, you'll have 48 inches remaining

(66 inches–18 inches). To the left of the sink base, you could fit a 21-inch-wide cabinet. That leaves 27 inches in the left-hand corner.

As you place cabinets consider the direction in which the doors should open. The most common arrangement is to have doors open away from the sink: The cabinets to the left of the sink would open to the left; those to the right would open to the right.

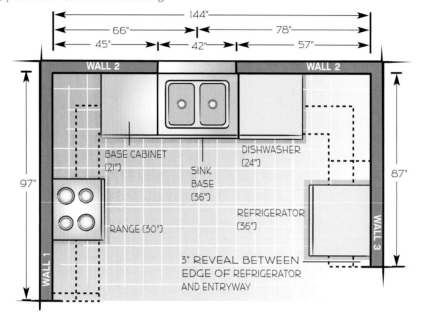

how much storage and counter space is enough?

CABINETS

- For kitchens smaller than 150 square feet, you need at least 156 inches of base cabinet frontage, 144 inches of wall cabinet frontage, and 132 inches of usable countertop length. Count only wall cabinets that are at least 30 inches high and 12 inches deep, and that have adjustable shelving; and base units that are at least 21 inches deep. You also need 120 inches of drawer or roll-out-shelf frontage (multiply the width of the units by the number of drawers or roll-outs).
- For kitchens larger than 150 square feet, you need 192 inches of base cabinet frontage, 186 inches of wall cabinet frontage, 198 inches of counter, and 165 inches of drawer or roll-out frontage. Count only cabinets 15 inches wide and 21 inches deep.
- Locate at least five storage units 15 to 48 inches above the floor. Include appliance garages, lowered wall cabinets, or raised base units.

- Within 72 inches of the center of the primary sink, you need 60 inches of wall-cabinet frontage.
- Include at least one corner cabinet.
- Include one waste bin and one recycling bin.

COUNTERS

- Consider two work-counter heights: one 28 to 36 inches off the floor, and the other 36 to 45 inches high.
- Include at least 24 inches of countertop length on one side of the primary sink, and 18 inches on the other.
- You need 9 inches of counter space on one side of the cooktop and 15 inches on the other, except at an end wall, where the minimum is 3 inches of clearance at the wall (and the wall must be covered by fire-resistant material).
- Beside the oven or the handle side of the refrigerator, you need 15 inches of counter space. The counter can be across from the appliance, provided it's no more than 48 inches away.

⑤ Choose Your Corner Cabinets

Start with the right-hand corner. Pick a corner cabinet that occupies 36 inches on each wall. In the left-hand corner, place a blind corner cabinet that takes up 24 inches on Wall 2. Fill in the 3-inch space that remains (27"–24"=3") with a 3-inch filler strip. These strips fill unused spaces and make it easy to open doors and drawers at corners and walls. (Buy a 6-inch filler strip and cut to size.)

Make sure the corner cabinets you choose will fit in the doorway. Check all doorways, hallways, and turns leading into the kitchen.

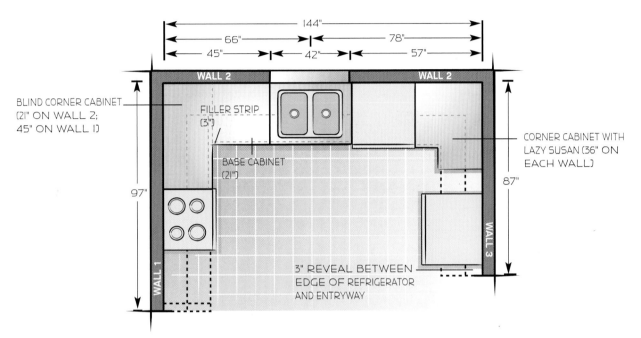

⑥ Choose the Base Cabinets Along the Remaining Walls

Start with Wall 3. The refrigerator, which is 36 inches wide, goes 3 inches from the entrance doorway. This leaves 12 inches for a cabinet between it and the corner unit (87"–3"–36"–36"=12").

Wall 1 has the range, which is 30 inches wide. The blind corner cabinet occupies 45 inches of wall space on Wall 1. The cabinet is 42 inches wide, but it needs to be placed 3 inches away from Wall 2 so it will align with the base cabinets on Wall 2. That leaves 22 inches for cabinet (97"–45"–30"=22") to the left of the range. Cabinets should fit next to the range unless you are using granite countertops, which require a little extra room. An 18-inch-wide cabinet between the range and the doorway leaves adequate clearance at the entry to the dining room.

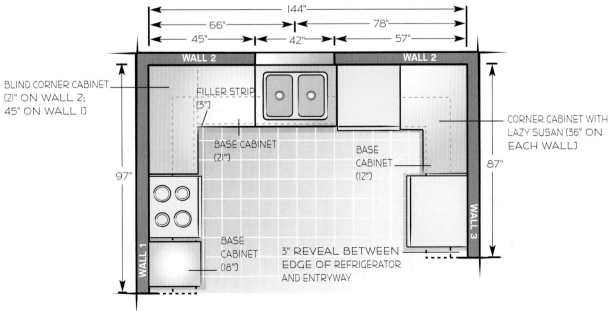

❼ Choose the Wall Cabinets

Placing the wall cabinets isn't much different from laying out the base units. The only difference is at the window. You can start placing cabinets only beyond the trim and, in this case, with an extra 3 inches on each side for blinds or curtains.

Wall 2 gets a cabinet 30 inches wide to the right of the window, and an 18-inch-wide unit to the left. A diagonal corner cabinet is placed in the right-hand corner; it occupies the remaining 24 inches of wall space on Wall 2 (57"–3"–30"=24"). A diagonal corner cabinet taking up 24 inches of wall space goes in the left-hand corner (45"–3"–18"=24").

On Wall 3 a 36-inch-wide cabinet goes above the refrigerator. With the 3-inch clearance between the cabinet and the doorway, and the 24 inches taken by the corner unit on Wall 2, we place a 24-inch-wide cabinet between the refrigerator and the corner (87"–36"–3"–24"=24").

On Wall 1 a 30-inch-wide cabinet goes above the range, and an 18-inch-wide cabinet goes to the left of the range. Taking the diagonal corner cabinet on Wall 2 into account, we place a 21-inch-wide cabinet next to the corner cabinet (97"–1"–18"–33"–24"=21"); this space can be taken by an above-the-range unit.

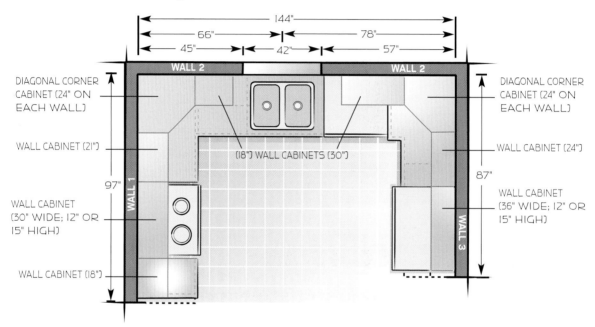

L-Shape Kitchens

Laying out an L-shape kitchen is almost the same as a U-shape one. The work triangle will be a little different. You won't be able to place the sink, range, and refrigerator on separate walls (as with the U). Two of them will have to go on the same wall. In this example, the sink is on one wall, centered under the window. The refrigerator is on the same wall, beside the kitchen entrance. The range is located on the adjoining wall.

Island Variation

If your layout includes an island, make sure there's enough space around it: 42 inches for a one-cook kitchen and 48 inches for two cooks. You can place either the sink or the range on the island. (There must be 9 inches of clearance between the back of the range and the edge of the counter.)

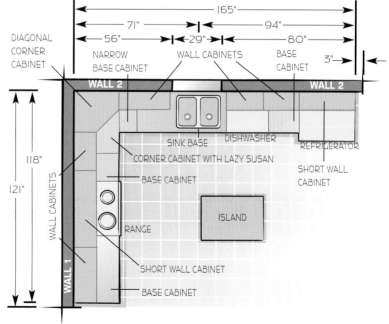

Galley Kitchens

A galley kitchen is much like a U-shape one, except you won't be able to draw your work triangle with the sink, refrigerator, and range on separate walls. In this example the sink goes near the middle of one wall under the window. The refrigerator and range are placed on the opposite wall: the refrigerator near the kitchen entrance, and the range near the other end.

One-Wall Kitchens

If your kitchen has one wall, you'll have to place all your appliances and cabinets on it. There's no work triangle. Place the sink between the range and refrigerator, with the refrigerator near the room entrance.

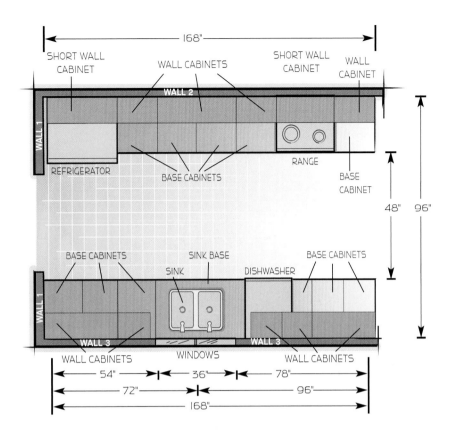

Elbowroom and Clearances

The NKBA guidelines covering adequate maneuvering space in the kitchen include the following:

- Make sure doorways are at least 32 inches wide.
- Put cabinets at least 36 inches away from the walls that they face. Put islands 42 inches from a cabinet— 48 inches if there are two cooks.
- Make sure entrance, cabinet, or appliance doors won't interfere with one another.
- In the eating area allow 36 inches of clearance around the table or counter—65 inches if the area will be a walkway. For a 30-inch-high table or counter, each diner needs 30 inches of elbowroom that is 19 inches deep, and 19 inches of knee space. For a 36-inch-high table or counter, allow for 24 inches (wide) and 19 inches (deep) of space, and 15 inches of knee space. For a 42-inch table or counter, the minimums are 24×12 inches, and 12 inches of knee space.
- Locate a dishwasher at least 21 inches from an inside corner, counter, cabinet, or appliance on an adjoining wall.

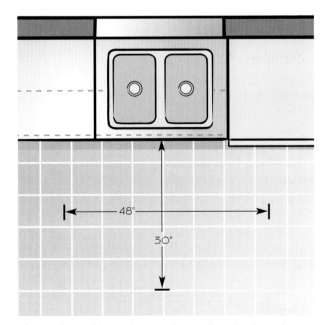

above To provide ample space for working at sinks and cabinets, allow a clear floor space of at least 30×48 inches.

Money Matters

A key part of the planning phase is establishing a detailed construction budget and balancing how much your plan will cost against how much you are willing to spend.

Minimize problems and headaches by keeping (and following!) a detailed budget. Make sure all elements, and the cost of each, are documented in your contract. Tracking costs will help you know if you will need to modify your wish list in order to stay on budget. Detailed estimates, including materials and labor breakdowns, help you set priorities and make trade-offs. Plan for a budget overrun of about 12 percent for unexpected problems.

Be Prepared for Anything

Construction costs, both materials and labor, vary significantly by region. Be prepared for the unexpected. Surprises are more likely to pop up in older homes where structural or mechanical problems could be be lurking. Changing the position of plumbing pipes and fixtures significantly increases your costs.

Is the Timing Right?

Evaluate whether sinking money into a major project at this time is a smart financial move.
- How old is your home?
- How long have you lived in your home?
- How long do you think you'll stay in your home?
- Have others in your neighborhood undertaken remodeling projects?

Resale value will influence design and product selections you make. If you plan to resell you will have to gear the look toward the mainstream at the cost of your personal taste. Research your neighborhood. Investigate schools and real estate values; see how properties are maintained. Talk with an agent to get an idea of recoupment on resale.

Budget Reducers

Compromises can save you money without sacrificing the overall plan. Seek the same designer look for a smaller price tag. Talk with your designer or other professional; browse magazines and home centers. Shop carefully for closeout models or discounted materials, and make sure parts are available.
- Would a major makeover, layout change, or bump-out do the trick at a much smaller cost?
- Must you change the location of the plumbing or electricity?
- Do you really need two sinks, and can you live with old appliances a little while longer?
- Can you do some of the work yourself?

How to Pay

Some homeowners choose to save and pay cash. Others take out a home equity loan, home equity line of credit, or second mortgage. Check out home centers that offer deferred billing and payments with no interest for proscribed time periods. Go online; you'll find many Web sites that walk you through various financial scenarios. Talk with different banks and mortgage companies or try a credit union. A major renovation is a significant expense. Make it a part of your overall financial planning.

avoid budget NIGHTMARES

Most projects will go over budget, but with careful planning (including adding in ample fudge room), you shouldn't be hit with too many unexpected surprises.

Problems often occur when homeowners:
- Take the lowest bid without checking references.
- Change their mind halfway through the project.
- Fail to specify brand and model names in the contract and the contractor passes on upgrades the homeowner didn't ask for.
- Are taken by complete surprise when major structural defects are discovered during the demolition phase.

Budgeting Your Kitchen

Recent numbers from the NKBA show that an average kitchen remodel runs about $27,000. A reasonable guideline is to keep the investment you make at 10–20 percent of the value of your home, but you may feel comfortable going higher if your home is in a higher price range. The NKBA provides the following budget summary information:

Cabinets	48%
Installation	16%
Countertops	13%
Appliances	8%
Design	6%
Flooring	4%
Plumbing fixtures and fittings	4%
Miscellaneous	1%

Only Averages

These are only averages. Be prepared to be surprised by the unexpected structural or mechanical problems—this is even more likely in older homes. Project and construction costs, including materials and labor, can vary significantly by region. Selecting custom cabinets, high-end appliances,

or solid-surfacing countertops or changing the plumbing will increase your costs and may result in significant changes to the average breakdown.

You can accomplish a minor fix-up with impressive cosmetic changes for a few thousand dollars, but a luxury expansion or redo can cost $50,000 or more. Have some informal discussions with contractors or local real estate agents to get a feel for costs and the features that are most popular among new home buyers. Many Web sites also provide a wealth of information about remodeling.

Watch out for extras. Sometimes to get the right look and features, you have to buy high-end products, but often cost is driven by extras you may not need or even want.

Average Costs

The following list of average item costs will help you build a budget. This chart does not include installation costs. Again, price ranges vary by region. Secure detailed price information by visiting stores, shopping online, and talking with builders, designers, and home center salespeople. When finalizing your budget, get an accurate picture with bids and estimates from professionals.

Item	Level	Cost	Considerations
Kitchen sink	Basic Mid-range High-end	$100–$200 $200–$400 $400–$4,000	The more expensive choices may include solid-surfacing materials, undermount installation, or apron-front style.
Kitchen faucets	Basic Mid-range High-end	$60–$150 $150–$200 $200–$600	More expensive choices include nicer finishes, pull-out sprayers, water purifiers, and perhaps wall-mount designs or features such as motion-sensor (no-hands) faucets.
Dishwashers	Basic Mid-range High-end	$300–$400 $600–$800 $1,000–$2,000	More expensive models may include pot-scrubbing and quiet cycles, built-in disposers, delayed wash and other features, water-heat boosters, or dishwashing drawers.
Vent hoods	Basic Mid-range High-end	$75–$150 $150–$1,000 $1,000–$5,000	The more expensive hoods may include downdraft vents, high-volume fans, stainless-steel housings, and professional-type or custom hoods.
Ranges	Basic Mid-range High-end	$300–$550 $550–$1,500 $1,500–$12,000	More expensive models may include self-cleaning and smooth-top glass or sealed gas burners, dual-fuel models, convection ovens, downdraft venting, grills, griddles, additional burners, and pro-style exteriors.
Cooktops	Basic Mid-range High-end	$300–$400 $400–$1,000 $1,000–$4,500	More expensive models may include smooth-top glass or sealed gas burners, continuous grates, electronic controls, front-panel controls, grills, griddles, woks, downdraft vents, and stainless-steel professional-grade models.
Ovens	Basic Mid-range High-end	$400–$750 $750–$1,200 $1,200–$4,600	Choices range from basic single models, either slide-in or built-in, to professional grade. Upgrades include self-cleaning features, convection, precision temperature controls, larger cooking capacity, closed-door broiling features, and professional-grade looks.
Microwaves	Basic Mid-range High-end	$80–$120 $200–$400 $600–$1,100	More expensive microwaves are typically built-in or over-the-range models.

Item	Level	Cost	Considerations
Refrigerators	Basic Mid-range High-end	$500-$700 $700-$2,000 $2,000-$7,000	More expensive options include freezer on bottom, side-by-side, or built-in with features such as automatic defrost, water and ice dispensers, separate temperature/humidity controls, digital temperature readout, and custom and adjustable shelves.
Trash compactors	Basic Mid-range	$350-$500 $500-$700	More expensive models are typically stainless steel.
Garbage disposers	Basic Mid-range High-end	$75-$100 $200-$350 $500+	More expensive models are higher power, quieter, continuous feed, and professional grade.
Cabinetry	Basic Mid-range High-end	$50-$150 per linear ft.	• Cabinets usually account for half the budget. • Stock cabinets cost $50-$200 per linear foot. • Semicustom cabinets can average two to three times more than stock cabinets. • Custom cabinets can cost up to five times more. • The more expensive cabinets may offer plywood or solid-wood materials (rather than particle board or veneer), tongue-and-groove construction, frame-and-panel designs, and sliding and specialty shelves and accessories.
Countertops (materials only)	Basic Mid-range High-end	$10-$50 per linear ft. $40-$150 per linear ft. $150+ per linear ft.	Basic: laminate, ceramic tile, stainless steel Mid-range: butcher block, concrete, solid-surfacing High-end: granite, marble • More expensive countertops offer more color selections; the more expensive materials include ceramic tile, butcher block, solid-surfacing, and certain stones.
Flooring (materials only)	Basic Mid-range High-end	$1-$5 per square ft. $3-$14 per square ft. $15-$30 per square ft.	Basic: laminate, vinyl tile, or vinyl sheet flooring Mid-range: ceramic tile, slate, or hardwood High-end: marble, granite, or limestone

Meet the Pros

Design and Planning Phase

■ Architects should be certified by the American Institute of Architects. They work with you from the beginning and draw up all of the plans and specifications. They also will review plans that have been prepared by others. If you are planning a major addition, an architect can help ensure it works with the style of your home.

■ Certified kitchen and bath designers must pass an exam to be certified by the NKBA (National Kitchen and Bath Association) and must fulfill continuing education requirements. They are qualified to both produce layouts and review plans prepared by other professionals. They can help supervise the contractor's work. In home centers, certified designers work with clients and supervise other employees in the design area.

■ Qualified interior designers provide planning and select materials, fixtures, elements, and colors. They can review plans and formulate design concepts. Some interior designers have a degree in interior design and are members of the American Society of Interior Designers. Some states also require that they be certified by the National Council of Interior Design.

Construction Phase

■ General contractors oversee the entire job. They hire and manage subcontractors who do specific work, such as plumbing or electrical installation. They get the correct building permits, schedule inspections, and ensure compliance with local building codes. They often offer design services as well. Hiring an experienced and reliable contractor is critical, especially if you're not using a designer.

■ Design-and-build firms offer both design and general contracting services. These firms typically have designers or architects on staff and also serve as building contractors. This can eliminate some of the headache of coordinating all the various professionals involved in a major project.

■ In addition to offering professional design services, most home centers will also work with you to arrange for the installation of many of the products you can purchase from them. Unlike many independent contractors that may take multiple "progress" payments over the course of the job, home centers may require full payment up front. However, the major home centers have every incentive to stand by their product and service offerings because the success of their businesses depends upon satisfied customers and positive word of mouth.

Hiring a Pro

If you need help planning and executing your remodel, hiring professionals is probably the answer. The type of pro you choose depends on your needs. Hire specialists only after looking carefully into their credentials and experience, and the associations they belong to. Certification and membership in professional organizations may signify commitment, but other professionals may be just as competent.

The True Tests

The true tests of designers or contractors are a portfolio of their work, an interview to see if there's a good fit, good word of mouth, and excellent references from satisfied clients.

Before you begin searching for professional help, address the following:

- Are you really ready to start building? Have you thought through your dreams for your new kitchen and settled on a design plan? A contractor will not be able to make an accurate estimate without a plan.
- Some contractors give rough estimates and provide initial consultations for free. Others are reluctant to give ballpark estimates in case their true bid is higher.
- Make sure you can make payments as they come due.

- See what adjustments may need to be made to your homeowner's policy during the construction phase and to cover the added value of the work being done.
- Make sure your new kitchen will be compatible with

all the other systems in your home such as HVAC, plumbing, and electrical. It may be worth an inspection by a qualified professional.

Get Recommendations

Be prepared to get bids for the job from at least three contractors and compare them carefully before you choose.

- Everybody has contacts for referrals, so don't be afraid to ask. Ask friends, relatives, neighbors, business colleagues, real estate agents, and bankers for referrals.
- Ask at your local home improvement store.
- Ask trade professionals who have provided good service in your home.
- Look for job-site signs in your neighborhood and keep an eye on the way the site is managed and cleaned up on a daily basis.
- Ask the designer or architect you are working with to recommend general contractors.
- Contact your local Better Business Bureau; check with national trade associations (including the National Association of Home Builders Remodelers Council, the National Association of the Remodeling Industry, and, for architect referrals, the American Institute of Architects) for local members.

What About a Contract?

Contracts are essential. You can consult an attorney or you can find sample contracts online or at office supply stores. The contract must include: a payment schedule, the start and completion dates, a detailed materials list, the total cost of the job, how changes will be handled, a warranty on materials and workmanship for one year, a request for lien release forms from the contractor and subcontractors at final payment, and an arbitration clause in case there are problems that can't be resolved through negotiation.

No matter who you choose to complete your installation, be sure to carefully review your contract so that you can be confident of the product and workmanship warranties and other guarantees that come with your purchase.

Payment Schedule

Spell out the total price of the job and the payment schedule. If full payment is required up front, make sure you review the contract carefully and understand the extent of guarantees and warrenties on products, installation, and materials. Otherwise, schedule a minimum of three payments. Pay 25 to 50 percent on signing, and make a second payment approximately halfway through the project. You could also make payments fixed to completion of phases. Always keep at least 20 percent of the total until the work is completed and you are completely satisfied.

COMMUNICATION is key

- After the work is under way visit the site as often as possible without becoming an annoyance. Establishing a good relationship with the contractor and the crew will inevitably pay off.
- Leave a notebook in a designated spot that you and the crew use to write notes, questions, and comments for each other.
- Have weekly review meetings with the contractor and the on-site supervisor. Address any concerns immediately. Speak up if the work is not satisfactory, if people who were not designated in the contract are working on-site, or if something does not seem right to you.
- Good communication involves both listening and speaking out.

CHAPTER 4

Shopping Guide

Sinks. Refrigerators. Faucets. Cabinetry. There are hundreds of products that provide service in a kitchen, so how do you make the right choices? This shopping guide will help you decide what's right for you.

CHAPTER 4 CONTENTS

left Choosing elements, the sinks, faucets, cabinets, countertops, appliances, and flooring that make up your kitchen presents an exciting prospect. But before taking off on a shopping adventure, go on a mini tour in this chapter. The photographs and information will help you make informed decisions that balance the budget, quality, and look suited to your kitchen design.

Sinks

Essential to food preparation, cooking, and cleanup, the kitchen sink gets a daily workout. That's why you need to choose a sink that is versatile and durable as well as stylish.

When deciding on a kitchen sink, focus on these key points:

- The size, depth, and number of bowls
- A mounting method appropriate for your sink and countertop
- The material that complements the design of your kitchen should stand up to wear and clean up well
- The style of your kitchen

The standard sink, with one bowl for washing and the other for rinsing, measures 33×22 inches. But one size does not fit all kitchens. Counter space dictates how large your sink should be. For example, in kitchens under 150 square feet, designers usually recommend a one-bowl sink that is 25×22 inches. Measure carefully: The size specifications provided by the manufacturer generally represent the inside of the bowl rather than the overall size of the unit. Measure the overall size when determining the amount of counter space you need.

Deeper Bowls Available

If buying just one sink, you can opt for a bowl depth of 10–12 inches over the conventional 8-inch depth. Deep sinks are capable of holding your largest pots and pans. Bear in mind, however, that a tall family member may find a deep sink requires more bending over. Raising the countertop a few inches may solve the problem. Talk it over before committing to a decision. Or if one cook is tall and the other short, installing two sinks—each at a comfortable height—is a worthy investment.

Try More Than One

If you have adequate space, regularly prepare family meals, and entertain often, consider larger models and a secondary sink. Given the rise in popularity of two-cook kitchens, snack zones within a kitchen, and islands designed for sinks, the secondary sink is no longer viewed as an unusual luxury. In fact, many families can't imagine functioning without it. Numerous options are available. A secondary sink can be smaller than the primary one, but bear in mind its purpose and choose size accordingly. For instance, if you want to wash and chop fresh vegetables and fruit, select a sink that is at least 13 square inches or slightly larger if it is round or oval.

More Than Two

If you have space, you might consider a triple-bowl sink. Two bowls for stacking dishes typically flank a small bowl for cleaning produce. Accessories galore often accompany these sinks: colanders, cutting boards, sink grids, fitted grids to protect glasses and fine china, and drainers. Some larger triple-bowl sinks include a ribbed drain board. But before splurging on a sink with accessories, think about your daily work routine and whether it warrants such an indulgence.

Sinks are available in a variety of shapes, including rectangular, oval, round, and asymmetrical. For visual interest, double or triple sinks may have a combination of shapes. Although attractive, a certain shape may present drawbacks. For instance, big pans may not lie flat in a sink with curved edges, compared to a same-size sink with square edges.

below A single-bowl sink works well in tighter spaces and offers a larger surface area. Single-bowl sinks are good choices if a secondary sink is part of the kitchen scheme.

above Apron sinks, also known as farmhouse sinks, are large, deep rectangular sinks with an exposed apron front. This style has regained popularity in recent years.

right Double-bowl sinks come in many materials and designs. This cast-iron model offers a slightly larger bowl on the left side as well as a hot-water dispenser, and the airgap for the dishwasher is on

Island Sinks

How you use your island determines the purpose of the sink. For example, if you have a cooktop on the island, a sink comes in handy for emptying a pot of hot water. That way you don't risk scalding yourself or a small child while carrying a pot across the room. If you lack counter space for a secondary sink, even a small island can accommodate it. Use it for prepping food or giving family members a place to wash up or get a glass of water.

Some local codes may not allow a sink to be installed in an island because venting the sink properly can be complicated. Check with local authorities in the early part of the design process to ensure that you will comply with local codes.

above If you use a secondary sink for food prep, such as scraping or cutting vegetables, make sure it is at least 13 inches square or a little larger if it is round or oval.

above Many designers suggest putting a sink at one end of the island, preferably near the refrigerator, rather than putting it in the center of the island, which cuts down on the available continuous workspace.

above If you desire a bar sink with a garbage disposal, make sure it is roomy enough to handle the food you are scraping and the scrap accumulating at the bottom.

above A set-in sink adds flair to a kitchen island. Just make sure the dimensions meet practical needs.

Sink Installation Options

Sink categories describe how a sink is installed and how it connects to and interacts with the countertop. The most common is the drop-in sink, which is mounted into the sink cutout from above and has a ridge that sits on the countertop. Self-rimming and rimmed sinks are examples of drop-in sinks. The second major category is an undermounted sink, which sits below the countertop and is attached to the underside of the sink cutout. The third category is an integral sink. The sink and countertop are one continuous piece of the same material. There are no joints or edges that catch crumbs.

above Self-rimming sinks are simply dropped into a hole cut into the counter. The rimmed edges of the sink sit on the countertop. The gaps between the rim and the countertop are caulked. Self-rimming sinks can be used with almost any type of available countertop material, and they can be replaced without moving the countertop or pipes. One disadvantage: The joint between the sink and the countertop requires regular cleaning.

above and below Integral sinks can be molded from the same material—such as solid-surfacing, stainless steel, and other stones so they have no visible joint between the sink and the counter. It's an easily cleaned surface and provides a contemporary look. However, if the sink becomes damaged, the entire piece has to be replaced.

left Undermount sinks are mounted from below the countertop. Cleanup is easy, as spills and crumbs from the counter can be wiped directly into the bowl. Undermount sinks must be used with materials that are waterproof from both sides, such as solid-surfacing, granite, and other stones. Laminate countertops cannot be used with an undermount sink.

Sink Materials

For general information on pricing see page 107.

Material	Description	Advantages	Disadvantages	Care
Stainless steel	The quality varies according to the gauge and nickel content, with the better styles being thicker and having a combination of nickel and chrome.	• Available in a variety of sizes and shapes • Lightweight, durable, and corrosion resistant • Moderate price • Popular for contemporary and professional-style kitchens	• Shiny surface show fingerprints, scratches, and water spots (brushed finishes show fewer marks) • Thin steel dents easily and shows scratches • Garbage disposer will cause vibrations, though 16- and 18-gauge sinks are thicker and less noisy	• Easy to clean • Thinner gauges are high maintenance
Enameled cast iron	Molten iron is poured into a mold and enamel coating is fired on.	• Provides a warmer, more traditional look • More substantial than stainless or enameled steel • Available in many colors • Stays shiny for many years • Quiet • Retains heat when washing dishes by hand • Today's materials less likely to chip than in the past	• More expensive than stainless or enameled steel • Very heavy so can be difficult to install • Dropped or banged glasses may break against it	• Easy to clean • Low maintenance
Enameled steel	Steel stamped or pressed into shape, covered with an enamel finish, and then furnace-fired; the enamel layer is thinner than that on enameled cast iron.	• Available in many colors • Resembles cast iron but is lighter and more flexible	• Thin and noisy • Doesn't stand up well to heavy use • Prone to chipping • Too flexible to support garbage disposers	• Easy to clean • Low maintenance
Composite	Usually a speckled color and made of granite, quartz, or other materials mixed with acrylic or polyester-resin base	• Durable • Available in many colors • Stands up well to hot spots • Nonporous and stain-resistant surfaces that feature color throughout	• Heavy knives can scratch or dent the surface • Expensive	• Easy to clean (avoid abrasive cleaner) • Low maintenance
Fireclay	Clay base fired at intense heat to produce finish	• Durable, even more so than enameled cast iron • Attractive glossy finish	• Limited variety of sizes and colors • Susceptible to chipping • Glasses and dishware break easily against it	• Low maintenance
Vitreous china	Clay coated with a fired-on glaze	• Hard • Nonporous • Glasslike shine • Resists moisture and mildew • Resists discoloration and corrosion	• May chip if struck by a heavy object	• Easy to clean
Solid-surfacing	Polyester or acrylic base usually integrated with solid-surfacing countertop	• Available in countless colors, from primaries to pastels • Resists scratches and chipping	• Specialized installation is required, which is more expensive • Susceptible to burns from hot pots and pans	• Easy to clean • Low maintenance • Used in integral sinks that have no joint or rim to trap food or dirt

Material	Description	Advantages	Disadvantages	Care
Soapstone	A light gray stone with a smooth soft texture that darkens with age	• Complements almost any design • Retains heat • Stands up to hot pots and pans	• Costs more	• Easy to maintain
Slate	Natural stone with an organic look	• Complements almost any design • Retains heat • Stands up to hot pots and pans	• Costs more	• Easy to maintain • Clean with warm, soapy water and rinse • Avoid abrasive cleanser or scrub pads
Granite	Natural stone that gives textured look	• Complements many designs • Retains heat • Stands up to hot pots and pans	• Costs more • Harder on dishes • Use restricted to hardest granite slabs that don't need sealing	• Clean with warm, soapy water and rinse • Avoid abrasive cleanser or scrub pads
Copper	With use assumes warm, weathered patina	• Complements natural materials of country style kitchen or metallic surfaces of contemporary setting • Finish may be hammered or smooth • Holds heat	• Expensive • Durable but soft and can be dented or scratched	• Clean with mild dish detergent and soft cloth, then rinse with water and wipe dry with clean, soft cloth
Brass	Imparts warm metal look	• Complements traditional design • Holds heat	• Expensive • Durable but soft and can be dented or scratched	• Clean with mild dish detergent and soft cloth, then rinse with water and wipe dry with a clean, soft cloth • Use professional brass cleaner to remove tarnish then wipe with clean, soft cloth

left This round stainless-steel sink would work well in a contemporary kitchen island. It's easy to clean and could have a disposer installed for convenience.

right The smooth finish of this copper sink has worn with use over the years, which gives it a more distinguished look.

left Adding color to an island countertop is easy with an enameled cast-iron sink.

Sink Fixtures

left and below A single-lever model offers a smooth, clean look along with ease of use and maintenance. Design options running from basic to ornate have made them increasingly popular.

Sink fixtures are more stylish and varied than ever. But to make a good investment, give equal attention to the internal-valve mechanism that governs the flow of water through the spout. Brass parts, being solid and heavy, withstand extreme temperatures. Beware of faucets with plastic shells or handles, despite their enticing lower price. They lack durability and resistance to scratching.

Valve Options

There are four basic types of faucet valve mechanisms: ceramic disk, cartridge, ball, and compression.

Ceramic-disk faucets have two ceramic disks that move against each other to block the flow of water. Generally more expensive, they're maintenance free.

Cartridge-type faucets, available in single- and double-handle configurations, are designed for easy repair. The flow mechanisms are contained in a cartridge that is replaceable when a leak occurs.

Single-handle ball faucets have a rotating ball inside the faucet. The ball moves over water-inlet holes, permitting water flow. It regulates the flow of hot and cold water, and shuts off water.

Compression faucets with double handles have been around for about 100 years. A rubber washer stems the flow of water. When the washer eventually becomes worn, the faucet tends to drip.

Installation Options

Installation options for faucets include: single-hole, center-set, widespread, and wall mount.

Single-hole models require just one hole on the sink ledge. They can have a single handle (usually connected to the spout) or hot- and cold-water handles.

Center-set faucets are one-piece fittings; the handles and spout are combined on a 4-inch base unit.

Widespread faucets separate the hot- and cold-water valves and the spout, giving more flexibility in placement. However, this model may cost twice as much as comparable center-set models.

Wall-mount faucets are mounted to the wall rather than the sink or countertop.

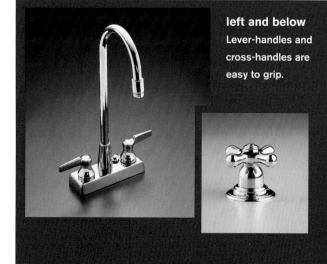

left and below Lever-handles and cross-handles are easy to grip.

Mounting Options

Most faucets are installed directly onto the sink or countertop. With undermount sinks, holes for the faucet are drilled directly into the countertop. With self-rimming sinks, the holes are in the sink. Make sure to match the number of holes you will need for your faucet with the number of holes drilled into the sink. If you end up with more holes in the sink or countertop than needed for the faucet you have selected, you can install a hot-water dispenser, liquid soap dispenser, or side sprayer over the holes. If your old sink has too many holes for your new faucet, cover the extra holes with a metal disk called an escutcheon plate. It's well worth the money and effort to purchase fixtures and a sink that are new.

One Handle or Two?

You'll need to decide between one- or two- handle fixtures. Here are some key points to consider:

- A single-handle faucet allows you to control volume as well as hot and cold water temperatures with one hand.
- A single-handle faucet is ergonomically sound. For example, you can turn it on with a wrist or elbow if your hands are covered with flour, batter, or grease.
- A single-handle faucet may require just one hole in the sink or sink ledge, making it easier to install.
- With one handle, a spout has a greater swinging radius.
- However, you may prefer a double-handle faucet, which offers a more traditional look. You also can independently control hot and cold temperatures with two handles.

above With a center-set unit, the spout and handle(s) are in a single unit. It also has a pullout sprayer built into the faucet. The retractable sprayer makes it easier to clean hard-to-reach areas of the sink, fill up large pots, and water nearby houseplants. The stainless-steel hoses offer better performance but are noisier going in and out.

Height and Shape

Next determine the height and shape of the spout appropriate for your needs and design requirements. Do you require the water to flow to hard-to-reach areas of a large sink? A faucet with an integral pullout sprayer or side sprayer may be in order. Do you often fill large pots? You may want to splurge on a high-arc faucet or separate pot filler mounted on the wall near your cooktop. Other accessories include dispensers for soap or lotion as well as a hot-water dispenser, a handy spout that delivers hot water instantly for coffee, soup, or tea.

left With spread-fit faucets, the handles and spout are separate units. Taller, longer spouts are becoming desirable because they offer more clearance for washing and filling large pots and pans and washing delicate glassware without banging it into the spout or against the sink's side or bottom. If you choose a double- or triple-bowl sink, evaluate the length and flexibility of the spout to ensure desired performance.

Instant Service

Most instant hot-water dispensers have half-gallon capacity. The heater is located under the sink or in the cabinet. When the faucet valve opens, unheated water enters the dispenser through the supply tube, heating as it passes through the expansion chamber. The pressure of the incoming water forces hot water from the holding tank and expansion chamber, where it cools to 200 degrees Fahrenheit, and out the spout.

Installation of a hot-water dispenser is not complicated. The most difficult step is adding an electrical receptacle under the sink. You can't use the same receptacle for your garbage disposer.

Chilled-water dispensers have the same basic design and can be a separate unit. Instead of having a heater, it has a chiller.

Some manufacturers offer a combined hot/chilled-water dispenser. A combined unit saves money and conserves space next to the sink and under the counter. The chilled water from a countertop dispenser is cool, but not as cold as that from a refrigerator door dispenser.

above Instant hot water is great for making that quick cup of soup, tea, or cocoa in the winter. It even comes in handy for blanching vegetables. If installed at the sink, a mini water heater is connected to the cold water supply beneath the sink. You can opt for a combination water dispenser that both heats and chills.

above Installed by the cooktop or range, a tall gooseneck faucet gives cooks the convenience of being able to fill a large pot with ease.

above and right
Wall- and side-mount faucets, which offer a different look, are seen in some contemporary kitchens. However, you can install traditional fixtures to create a vintage look. Wall-mount faucets allow for more open space on the counter.

Fixture Materials

Traditional chrome and brass finishes continue to be popular, but they have been joined by a wide selection ranging from muted metal tones to baked-on epoxy. Improvements in applying the finishes have been made, leading to many styles and materials that are durable and easy to clean.

When selecting a finish, some people choose to match the fixture finish to the sink, countertop, or appliances. Personal preference may lead you to polished chrome or brass, or you may lean toward the more muted finishes that blend well with popular stainless-steel appliances. Many people like the look of a matte faucet finish that complements surfaces made of wood, stone, tile, or other natural material. For general infromation on pricing see page 107.

Material	Advantages	Disadvantages	Care
Chrome (polished, brushed, or matte finish)	• Chrome is common • Polished chrome is inexpensive, hard, and does not oxidize • Matte chrome has a softer appearance and is very durable	• Chrome over inexpensive plastic parts will peel	• Easy to clean • To keep shine, clean often
Colored (baked on enamel or epoxy coating)	• Wide choice of deep, rich colors	• May chip • Can fade in sunlight, although epoxy finishes are tougher than enamel finishes • Prone to chemical change	• Easy to clean
Nickel (polished or brushed finish)	• Traditional appeal • Quality metal resists tarnish • Matte finish hides scratches, water spots, and fingerprints	• Quality varies	• Clean with warm, soapy water
Brass (high gloss, satin, or antique finish)	• Classic look • Those with titanium finish resist scratching, fading, and corrosion	• Standard brass finishes are prone to corrosion, scratching, and tarnishing unless a protective coating has been applied	• Polish frequently with soft cloth to remove water spots and soap film • Shine with rubbing alcohol
Copper (polished or brushed finish)	• An old-fashioned look and simple beauty • Titanium-strengthened copper has a very durable finish	• Expensive • Quality varies • Requires finish by manufacturer or finish may damage	• Clean with mild dish detergent and soft cloth; then rinse with water and wipe dry with a clean, dry cloth • Use professional copper cleaner to remove tarnish, then wipe with clean, soft cloth
Pewter (polished or brushed finish)	• Visual appeal • Quality metal resists tarnish • Matte finish hides scratches	• Expensive • Quality varies	• Clean with warm, soapy water
Gold plate	• Visual appeal • If good quality, the metal resists tarnish • Matte finish hides scratches	• Expensive • Quality varies • Requires finish sealed by manufacturer or the gold may become damaged	• Clean with warm, soapy water

Cabinets

Kitchen cabinets can consume up to half of your kitchen remodeling budget and greatly influence the style of your kitchen, so they are well worth understanding inside and out.

Cabinet Types

Cabinets fall into three basic categories, depending on how they're constructed and whether they can be customized. They are stock, built-to-order, or custom-made. There are two basic styles of construction—framed and frameless. (See pages 124–125.)

Stock Cabinets

- Sold fully assembled or ready to assemble (RTA).
- They are typically constructed of particleboard with doors, drawers, and face frames made of hardwood.
- Generally the least expensive, they're mass-produced.
- They're available in a standard range of styles and sizes.
- Stock units are made in 3-inch-wide increments (the smallest is 9 inches wide and the largest 48 inches; the units increase in size by 3-inch increments).
- Typically, those less than 24 inches wide have one door, and wider ones are designed with two doors.
- The quality can be excellent, but material and accessory options may be limited.

Built-to-Order (Semi-Custom)

- These cabinets are midrange in terms of both cost and options.
- They are built by a manufacturer to a limited range of specifications, with more design flexibility than stock cabinets (more choices in cabinet sizes, certain types of interior fittings, such as pullout shelves and lazy Susans, as well as a variety of door styles, hardware, and finishes).
- Materials tend to be a higher grade than those used in stock units and include medium-density fiberboard (MDF), which is superior to particleboard, better-quality wood veneers, and durable varnishes.
- You may wait from 3 to 12 weeks for delivery, depending on the complexity of the job.

Custom

- These cabinets are usually the most expensive option.
- They are built to suit specific needs, with the work often done by local cabinetmakers, though some factory-made

lines will allow you to order a custom kitchen. It's possible to order custom cabinets through kitchen dealers and home centers.
- If you want to keep some of your existing units, a custom cabinetmaker can produce new ones to match.
- If you need to solve an unusual layout problem that can't be solved with stock or built-to-order products, custom cabinets offer an answer.
- You can select the material of your choice: solid wood or plywood, MDF, or particleboard covered with laminate or wood veneer.

inspect the CABINETS

Inspect your cabinets for damage **on delivery**! Don't wait until the installer arrives to open the boxes. Damaged cabinets guarantee delays while waiting for replacements.

Standard Cabinet Dimensions

Use these dimensions for stock kitchen cabinets as a reference. Read product information carefully because not every manufacturer will have every size listed below.

Base Cabinets

Base cabinets are those units that sit on the floor, including sink base units and a variety of specialty units.

- The height of standard base units is 34½ inches (this height includes the toe-kick, which is the 3-inch recess along the bottom front of the cabinet).
- The standard depth is 24 inches.
- The width ranges from 9 to 48 inches (in 3-inch increments).
- Units with a single drawer over a door typically vary in width from 12 to 24 inches, while units with double doors and a single shelf typically range in width from 27 to 48 inches.
- Base units can have doors, drawers, or a combination of the two, with the most common types having a single drawer over a single door.
- Most cabinet manufacturers offer base units with a variety of accessories, such as lazy Susan and pullout trash and recycling centers.
- Sink units are typically 24 to 48 inches wide with two doors and false drawer fronts.
- Specialty units include blind-corner base cabinets, diagonal and corner sink base units, corner cabinets with a lazy Susan, wall-oven cabinets, and a variety of other utility cabinets.

Wall Cabinets

Wall cabinets run along the wall; some go in the corner or over the oven. A variety of specialty units are available.

- The available heights for standard units are 12, 15, 18, 24, 30, 36, and 42 inches.
- The most common units are 30 inches high with two adjustable shelves.
- The depths are 12, 15, 18, 21, and 24 inches (the most typical is 12 inches deep).
- The widths range from 9 to 48 inches in 3-inch increments.
- One-door units are typically 9 to 24 inches wide, while two-door units are typically 24 to 48 inches wide.
- Wall cabinets almost always have doors.
- Specialty units include blind-corner cabinets, pie-cut corner cabinets, diagonal corner cabinets, and cabinets built to hold microwave ovens.

Oven Cabinets

- The heights are 84, 90, and 96 inches.
- The depth is 24 inches.
- The widths are 24, 27, 30, and 33 inches.

Utility Cabinets

- The standard height is 84, 90, or 96 inches.
- The depth is 12, 18, or 24 inches.
- The widths are 12, 15, 18, 24, 30, and 36 inches.

Framed (or Face-Framed) Cabinets

Framed cabinets have been around for centuries and are more traditional. The exposed edges of the frame (the "reveal") are visible around the doors and drawers.

- This cabinet has the most traditional look and type of construction.
- The face frame is attached to the front of the cabinet box.
- The frame is purposely made to be slightly wider than the cabinets. When two cabinets are placed together, the frames form a tight seam when installed properly.
- The frame reinforces the box, and the doors are hung from it with exterior hinges that are attached to both the face frame and the inside face of the door.
- The hinges attaching the doors to the frame may be either exposed or hidden.
- The cabinet sides fit into the face-frame stile and are glued, nailed, or stapled into place.
- The cabinet typically includes removable shelves that rest on adjustable brackets.
- Stock framed cabinets can come as wide as 48 inches (custom cabinets can be even wider).
- The frames make the box opening smaller.

Framed Wall Cabinet

- Cabinet sides fit into the face-frame stile and are glued and nailed or stapled into place.
- Cabinet bottoms and tops fit into grooves in the sides.
- Shelves are often fixed; removable shelves rest on adjustable brackets.
- Doors are attached with exterior hinges that are attached to the face frame and the inside of the door face.

Framed Base Cabinet

- Corner blocks are screwed to the mounting rail and the sides of base cabinets. They help square the cabinets and provide mounting surface for countertops.
- Framed cabinets usually are attached to the wall with a mounting rail at the back of the cabinet. Shelves may be fixed but can also be adjustable.
- Drawer box fronts are often covered with false fronts, which are screwed to the box. The false front is usually larger than the drawer front and overlays the face frame around the drawer opening.

Frameless Cabinets

Compared to framed cabinets this cabinet type is a relatively recent development, offering a more contemporary look.

- There is no face frame; rather, a hinge supports a door nearly as wide as the cabinet.
- Access is easier, with slightly more space inside.
- Shelves are usually adjustable.
- A roll-out shelf can take up the entire width of the cabinet.
- Until installed, frameless cabinets are less rigid than framed; but if installed squarely, they are very solid as they are supported by one another and the kitchen wall.
- A design that uses a frameless cabinet may need to allow for additional door clearance, which may require using filler strips and overlay fillers.
- Frameless cabinets are commonly made of laminate, but furniture-grade plywood is also available.

Frameless Wall Cabinet

- Interior hinges are concealed on the inside face of the cabinet side of the door and are adjustable to square doors over their openings.
- There are predrilled holes for hinges, shelf supports, and drawer runners.
- Shelf pins fit in predrilled holes in cabinet sides to support adjustable shelves.

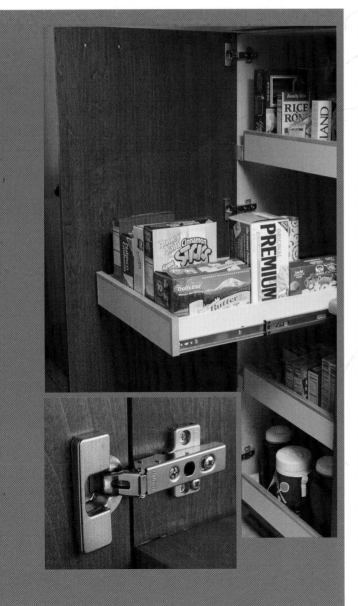

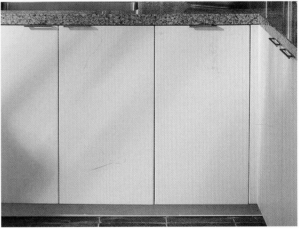

Frameless Base Cabinet

- Doors attach to one side of the cabinet box.
- Shelves are usually adjustable.
- Corners are often joined with wooden dowels.
- Most North American cabinets are leveled with shims. (Leveling legs are common in Europe.)
- Drawers open and close smoothly on glides fastened to the cabinet sides.
- Rubber bumpers muffle the noise of closing doors and drawers and prevent marring.

Cabinet Anatomy

Understanding the different cabinet parts will help you make the best selection. After reviewing this information, start browsing. Don't rush your decision.

Here are the types of substrates used in most cabinets:

Particleboard

- This substrate is made of wood particles mixed with resin and bonded under pressure.
- Cabinet interiors are often made of particleboard, particularly cabinetry that will be covered with laminate and vinyl film.
- Advances in manufacturing have improved its strength and reliability, but watch out for poor grades.

Medium-Density Fiberboard (MDF)

- This high-quality material is made from finer fibers than those used in particleboard.
- The surface is much smoother.
- The edges can be shaped and painted.
- This substrate offers superior screw-holding power.

Plywood/Engineered Wood

- These substrates are made by laminating thin layers of wood plies onto each other.
- The grain of one layer is run at right angles to the grain of the previous layer, giving plywood equal strength in all directions.
- The layers are bonded with glue under heat and pressure.
- Thin plywood is often used for cabinet backs; thicker plywood is used for cabinet sides.
- Veneers are available.

Cabinet Surface Materials

The variety of materials used as cabinet finishes fall into two primary categories: laminates and wood veneers. A laminate surface is made of three resin-saturated layers (a base layer of paper, a printed and colored layer, and a protective transparent layer). Heat and pressure fuse the laminate to the substrate. Choices in color, pattern, and quality vary widely. Here is an overview of common laminate options.

- High-pressure laminates provide vertical surfaces with the same durability as countertops, but they are more expensive.

frame of REFERENCE

As you inspect cabinets and talk over decisions with professionals, you'll want to know basic construction terms.

- **Biscuit joint:** a joint held together by thin wooden ovals that are embedded between the two pieces to be seamed with a special joiner. Commonly used to hold post form laminate countertops together.
- **Center stile:** the middle strut in a framed cabinet (also called a mullion).
- **Cross member:** a horizontal support in a frameless cabinet.
- **Dado joint:** a joint between two pieces of wood where one piece fits into a notch, or dado, cut in a second piece.
- **Dovetail joint:** an interlocking corner joint where pins on one piece fit into sockets on a second piece.
- **Dowel pegged joint:** a joint held together with dowel pins.
- **Filler:** a strip of wood placed between cabinets at corners to ensure doors and drawers open freely; it also fills gaps between the cabinet and the wall or helps set the cabinet plumb and level.
- **Intarsia:** a decorative groove cut into the top and bottom of cabinets; the top groove can replace a doorknob or handle.
- **Rabbet:** a wood joint in which one piece fits into a groove cut along the edge of the other piece.
- **Rail:** a horizontal crosspiece in a cabinet face frame or door (a rail at least $\frac{3}{4}$ inch thick helps solidify cabinets).
- **Reveal:** on a framed cabinet, the distance between the edge of the face frame and the edge of the door usually $\frac{3}{16}$ to $\frac{1}{4}$ inch.
- **Shim:** a thin, wedge-shaped piece of wood used to fill gaps between a cabinet and the wall to level the unit.
- **Stile:** a vertical piece of cabinet face frame or door.

- Low-pressure laminates, also called melamine, are less impact resistant than high-pressure laminates and have a tendency to crack and chip, but use of better substrates can reduce these problems.
- Resin-impregnated foils and heat-stamped transfer foils come in wood grains and some solid colors. The heavier the weight, the better the scuff resistance. These laminates generally are applied to cover curves and contours. The seams are undetectable.
- Thermofoil is a vinyl film applied to a substrate with heat and pressure. It more closely resembles wood than other laminates. It's easy to care for and less likely to chip than painted cabinets.

Selecting Wood Veneer

Wood veneer comes from peeling strips of wood off a tree. Thinner than solid wood, it's adhered to plywood or particleboard. Available on higher-end cabinets, wood veneer gives them warmth and texture. When selecting a wood veneer, assess the grain, density, and color, but remember that wood can be treated with a variety of stains to achieve different looks. For example, a stain can replicate the look of maple on a birch base.

Door Styles

The look of cabinet doors makes a strong first impression, contributing to the overall kitchen design. Although many varieties exist, they fall into two primary categories: slab and frame-and-panel. Solid wood doors will have natural variations including knots and mineral streaks.

Slab Doors

- Its clean lines offer a more contemporary look.
- Slab doors are typically made of several pieces of wood glued together, giving the appearance of a single panel of wood.
- These doors are most often used in the frameless style.

Frame-and-Panel Doors

- The panels are set in grooves inside the frame, giving the wood room to swell or shrink with humidity. If the panels were glued to the frame, the door might crack or warp.
- In a combination door, the frame consists of lumber and the panel of plywood.
- If the panel is flat, the door is referred to as a recessed-panel door.
- If the center of the panel is raised, the door is referred to as a raised-panel door.
- If glass, metal, or another type of insert is used rather than a wood panel, it is secured against an open lip on the back, not within the frame.

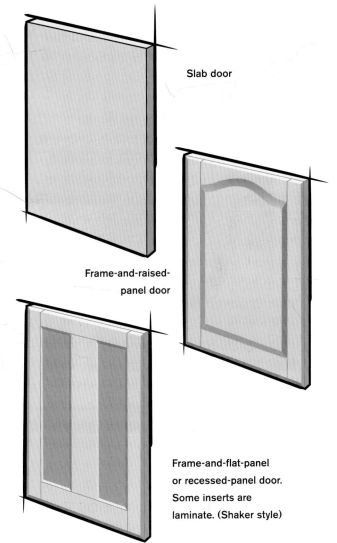

Slab door

Frame-and-raised-panel door

Frame-and-flat-panel or recessed-panel door. Some inserts are laminate. (Shaker style)

left Cabinet doors are available in many styles that will vary by vendor and dimension, although most fall into a few main categories. Three of the most common variations—an aptly named slab door and two popular frame-and-panel doors—are shown above.

The Core of the Cabinet: The Box and the Drawers

Spend plenty of time looking at cabinets and you'll soon develop an eye for quality. Take your time looking. Here are some points to keep in mind:

- The best wood cabinets have solid doors with grain running in the same direction on exposed sides, backs, drawer fronts, doors, and shelves.
- Drawer construction varies by manufacturer. Quality drawers can also be made of metal or engineered wood.
- Drawers are made of solid wood or plywood.
- The side panel, back panel, and floorboard of a cabinet are typically made of plywood, particleboard, or MDF that has been covered with veneer.
- Less expensive cabinets have doors and frames of plywood, veneered particleboard, or wood-grain laminate.

- Regardless of material the door and drawer edges should be smooth to the touch.
- The best joint for a cabinet box is a dado joint, in which the sides fit into grooves that have been cut into the cabinet back and the face frame. Dado joints are more stable than those that have been butted and glued.
- Corner gussets—triangular braces glued into the upper corners of the cabinet box—add strength.
- The back panel adds strength and guards against invasion by insects and vermin.
- Plastic clips hold false drawer fronts in place.
- Because wood warps easily it's best for wood cabinets to be finished before they leave the factory or cabinetmaker. If they arrive unfinished, finish them as soon as they are installed.

Adjustable metal hinges help align doors on frameless cabinets.

A close look at individual components can reveal much about the quality of kitchen cabinets. Well-constructed drawers are the best indication of fine quality: Look for interlocking joinery, thick bottoms, and smooth-running slides.

Rails at least ¾ inch thick help solidify cabinets.

Cabinet Shelves

- Look for shelves that are made from ¾-inch high-grade particleboard that has been covered with veneer.
- Adjustable shelves are usually held in place with easily movable pins or clips that have been inserted into holes drilled along the inside of the cabinet box.
- Many cabinets now come equipped with roll-out trays, which are a cross between a drawer and a shelf. These should be installed with the same high-quality slides recommended for drawers.

Types of Cabinet Wood

Hard Maple

- Popular in semicustom or custom cabinetry
- Fine, straight grain and light color
- Stable and durable
- Slightly more expensive than oak

Red Oak

- Used in stock or semicustom cabinetry
- Often used to create a traditional look
- Strong, durable, and relatively inexpensive
- Pronounced grain patterns, open grain

Birch

- Used in stock or semicustom cabinetry
- Slightly darker than maple
- Can be stained to achieve the look of cherry or maple
- Durable or fine-grain wood

Cherry

- Used in stock or semicustom cabinetry
- Stands up well to heavy use
- Darkens with age, so is usually stained to ensure uniformity of color
- Used in traditional and contemporary styles

Pine

- Usually used in semicustom cabinets
- The only soft wood recommended for cabinets. Often has maple frame for extra rigidity
- Can be stained
- Used in traditional and country styles

Ash

- Used in custom and some semicustom cabinets
- Similar in strength and durability to oak
- Lighter than oak
- Often used in contemporary styles

Hickory

- Used in custom or semicustom cabinets
- Lighter in color than oak
- Can be stained but works best with clear or natural finish
- Wild graining with knots works best with rustic styles

White Oak

- Generally used only in custom cabinets
- Slightly stronger than red oak
- Durable

How Doors Fit

Now that you have an idea of the cabinet type that you want to grace your kitchen, here are different types of cabinet doors that are available. How a door fits over the cabinet box determines its classification.

Partial Overlay

■ The door is large enough to cover the opening, but small enough to reveal the cabinet's frame.

■ It is the least expensive and easiest to construct.

Full Overlay

■ The door covers the face frame (or the entire box front on frameless cabinets).

■ Only a sliver of space exists between doors and drawers.

■ Only full overlay is used on frameless cabinets.

Flush inset

■ The doors and drawers fit flush with the face frame.

■ A precision fit is available only in custom cabinets.

Lipped

■ To fit over the face frame, the door is routed with a wooden groove.

Framed

Frame up. In framed cabinets, doors may be flush with the front face of the frame or overlay it. In partial overlays, the edges of the door reveal part of the frame. In full overlay doors, the doors sit on the front stiles of the cabinets.

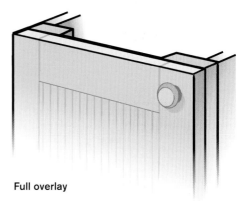

Flush-inset

Full overlay

Frameless

Clean lines. On frameless cabinets, recessed doors sit flush with the front edge of the cabinet sides. Full-overlay doors sit on the front of the cabinets. These options are available in framed cabinets as well.

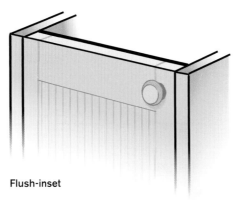

Flush-inset

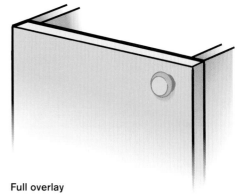

Full overlay

Drawers

You can easily determine overall quality by examining drawer construction. Also test the drawers. Check how smoothly the drawer moves in and out, and make sure you can easily access the interior.

Drawer Fronts

The visible part of the drawer is constructed two ways.

■ An inset, or flush front, drawer closes so that its face is flush with the surrounding cabinet.

■ An overlay drawer has a false front screwed to the drawer. It extends past the edges and top of the drawer front.

Solid Drawer Bottom

■ Look for ½- or ¾-inch solid wood sides and a plywood bottom panel at least ³⁄₁₆ inch to ¼ inch thick that has been glued into grooves.

■ Thinner bottoms (⅛ inch thick) may buckle under the weight of heavy loads.

■ Make sure bottoms are set in the routed grooves of all four sides.

■ Solid wood bottoms may float to accommodate expansion and contraction caused by changes in humidity, but plywood bottoms are often glued.

Quiet, Smooth Slides

Cabinet drawers usually are mounted on metal slides. Look for quality drawers. Here are some tips:

above Extended drawers that support heavy loads, such as this recycling bin, require sturdy slides that will not only hold the weight when closed but also at full extension.

■ Quality slides are rated to support at least 75 pounds.

■ You should be able to pull out a drawer easily and silently whether opening it partially or all the way.

■ Full-extension slides, which attach to the bottom or sides of the drawer and have a ball-bearing system, allow full access to the inside of the drawer. Make sure they have stops so they don't roll out. Although more expensive, they offer stability. You can store cookware in drawers with full-extension slides.

■ Solid metal slides with ball-bearings have bumpers to cushion the impact of the drawer as it closes. Their runners mount to the bottom of the drawer.

■ Nylon rollers on steel tracks attach to the sides of drawers. They're quiet but not as reliable as slides with ball bearings.

■ When a drawer is opened an inch, it should close on its own.

■ Side-mount glides are more common, but drawers with a bottom-mount mechanism save space on both sides and offer a higher-quality look.

■ Special pull-through slides, allowing a drawer to open from either side of a cabinet, are useful on a kitchen island.

■ Other glides have releases so you can remove drawers from cabinets for cleaning.

Cabinet Hardware

Knobs and Pulls

Cabinet hardware should be functional, but it should also affect the overall style. Note that hardware doesn't come with the cabinetry and the holes are not predrilled. Knobs and pulls are available in home centers, hardware stores, and even department stores. Shop catalogs and online, as well as flea markets and antique stores.

- Knobs on roll-out pantries and other heavy-duty items should be easy to grasp, sturdy, and comfortable to use.
- Styles are almost endless: reproductions from certain periods, unusual shapes reflecting special interests or hobbies, shapes to complement the cabinet styles and other decorative features of the kitchen.

- Materials selections include glass, wood, resin, ceramic, metal (including nickel, pewter, chrome, bronze, and iron), rubber, and stone.

Hinges

- Hinges can be visible, partially visible, or hidden.
- With visible hinges choose a style that blends with the other cabinet hardware.
- Invisible hinges fit both framed and frameless cabinets, allow for different opening and closing options, and are fully adjustable.

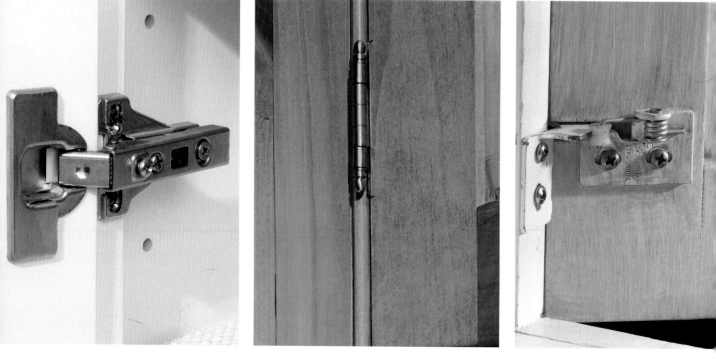

Storage Options

You'll want to use every inch of storage space in your kitchen cabinets. The number and variety of accessories are astounding. Make storage part of your remodeling plan. Home centers are sources of good advice about efficient storage. Consider accessories that keep your kitchen organized and minimize stooping, bending over, and reaching. Following are some kitchen storage options.

Wire under-shelf storage

Divided vertical storage for flatware

Slide-out towel rack

Slide-out storage trays

Door-mounted pantry

Pull-down undersink storage

Slide-out pantry

Built-in pantry

Divided cookware drawers

Wicker storage baskets on open shelving

Slide-out work counter

Slide-out recycling and trash center

Appliance garage

Pull-down cabinet shelving

Revolving storage trays in corner cabinet

Knife storage with cutting board

Recipe storage in a cabinet file drawer

Built-in spice drawer

Countertops

Many of today's kitchens mix and match countertop materials creating both a distinctive look and enhancing functionality such as heat-resistant materials by the cooktop and a cool marble surface in the baking center.

Edges can be an integral part of the countertop or can be added molded pieces. Solid-surfacing countertops can be worked just like wood to create a variety of edging shapes.

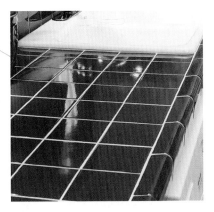

Laminate

Laminate is made of thin layers of plastic bonded to a core of plywood or particleboard. Laminates are available in a multitude of colors, finishes, and textures.

Solid-Surfacing

These countertops are made from polyester, acrylic resins, or a combination of both. Solid-surfacing countertops must be professionally installed to guarantee the warranty.

Ceramic Tile

You can use either floor or wall tiles for countertops. For countertops that will see heavy use, such as in the food preparation center, the more durable floor tiles are recommended.

Material	Advantages	Disadvantages	Care
Laminate	• Durable • Stain resistant • Wide variety of colors and finishes • DIY installation	• Knives and hot pans can mar low-end models • Glossy finishes may look great when new but tend to show dirt and scratches over time • Cannot be repaired if damaged, burned, or stained	• Low maintenance
Solid-surfacing	• Very durable • Customization is available • Available in many colors, patterns, and finishes • Surfaces can mimic granite and other stones • Less expensive and easier to install than granite • Color is solid throughout • Most damage can be repaired	• Professional installation • Knives can scratch the surface • Hot pans can burn the surface • A high-gloss finish on a dark counter can show scratches and nicks	• Easy to clean • Shallow cuts can be sanded out with an abrasive pad
Ceramic tile	• Durable • Available in many shapes, sizes, patterns, and colors • Stock tiles are comparable in price to laminate • Moisture resistant • Stands up to hot pots and pans • DIY installation	• Slightly uneven surface due to grout lines, which makes it a poor chopping surface • Custom and hand-painted tiles are more expensive	• Glazed tiles are easy to clean • Grout line is easily stained and can be difficult to keep clean

Stone Tile and Slabs

These are natural stones such as marble, limestone, slate, soapstone, lavastone, sandstones, granite, or marble tiles. Select larger slabs so there will be fewer seams in the countertop.

Butcher Block or Hardwood

The surface is created by laminating hardwood strips. It is best used in a small-area prep center.

Quartz Surfacing

A stone counter surface made of 93 percent natural quartz along with binders and pigments creates more consistent color and higher performance than other natural stones.

Material	Advantages	Disadvantages	Care
Stone tile and slabs	• Extremely durable • Consider granite or marble tiles (less expensive and easier to handle than slabs of stone) • Marble is an excellent choice for a baking center • Granite is less porous than marble, is stain- and scratch-resistant, and can stand up to hot pans, water, and knives	• Expensive • Heavy and difficult to install • Marble stains easily and is not a good choice for an entire countertop but works well for a pastry counter	• Dark, glossy colors of granite can be difficult to clean • Marble should be resealed frequently • Granite and marble should be sealed and polished on a regular basis
Butcher block or hardwood	• Excellent cutting surface • Some damage can be smoothed out with sandpaper	• Can be damaged by water	• High maintenance • Should be cleaned thoroughly following food preparation • Apply finishing oil frequently
Stainless steel	• Durable • Heat resistant, good choice next to a cooktop • Does not stain • Great professional look when matched with stainless-steel appliances	• More difficult to install • Scratches easily • Some find it noisy	• Easy to clean
Cast concrete	• Durable • Can be finished to be smooth or textured • Available in many colors	• Must be sealed frequently • Pricey • Installation is time intensive	• When sealed, the surface is easy to clean • Glossy surfaces clean most easily
Soapstone	• It stands up well to hot pots and pans and does not stain	• It is soft, so it is prone to scratches	• Should be sealed periodically with mineral oil
Quartz surfacing	• High performance • Consistent color • Variety of colors available • Durable	• Installation can be time intensive.	• Easy to clean with soap and water • Resists stains

countertop TIMING

Solid surface, quartz surface, and natural stone countertops require a template be made on site to ensure a good fit. Add time to the installation schedule and assume that you will use temporary tops until the top is finished.

Appliances

Refrigerators

You will find that there are refrigerators to fit every budget, and that today's models are more energy efficient and environmentally friendly than ever. When shopping for a refrigerator, first consider the amount of cold storage capacity you need. To determine the total amount of cold storage capacity, think about how much you cook and entertain, how often you shop for groceries, and whether you own a separate freezer.

How Much Room?

As a general guideline, allow for 12 cubic feet of storage space (counting both refrigerator and freezer space) for two people and add 2 more cubic feet per additional person who lives with you. You do not want to pay for more space than necessary, but be realistic. A refrigerator crammed with items has limited air circulation and costs more to run. Make sure doors can open fully so bins and shelves can be easily removed for cleaning.

Coordinate Surfaces

If you want the refrigerator door to coordinate with countertop surfaces, cabinetry, or other appliances, you can request appropriate door panels in some models. Finishes vary from standard pebble to a glasslike finish to more expensive stainless steel. There are new finishes available that mimic stainless steel but resist smudges and fingerprints.

Figure the Operating Cost

When pricing refrigerators, it's important to consider operating costs too. Read the yellow energy guide label on models you are considering. Balance the cost of any extras against how often you will use them. Models with all the options or with customized front panels are more expensive.

Also think through the major categories (side-by-side, top or bottom freezer, built-in,). Weigh which is best for your kitchen: a freestanding or built-in unit or a cabinet depth unit that can give the appearance of a built-in.

Top-mounted refrigerators are perhaps the most common choice of homeowners. Usually the least expensive option, it operates efficiently. However, some shorter adults and children find it difficult to reach items in the back of the freezer, and taller adults have to bend to reach some items in the refrigerator section.

Bottom-mounted refrigerators cost more than top-mounted models, but offer easier access to both the main cold storage area and the freezer compartment. Most bottom-mounted models have roll-out shelves or bins in the freezer area. In some the entire freezer section pulls open like a drawer.

Side-by-side refrigerators offer eye-level access to both the refrigerator and freezer. When the narrow doors open, they take up less clearance space in the kitchen. However, the doors and shelves may not hold some large containers and bulky frozen items.

refrigerator
FEATURES

Refrigerators offer all sorts of features and conveniences. Look them over carefully, weighing how important they are on a daily basis:

- Automatic defrost
- Additional insulation
- Digital displays
- Adjustable deep-door bins that hold 2-liter containers and 1-gallon jugs.
- Sliding brackets to secure bottles and jars (some models have wine racks)
- Spill guard (raises the border on glass shelves)
- Glass shelves for easy cleaning
- Shelves that fold away to accommodate large or tall products
- Top shelves that adjust with a crank
- Half shelves that adjust to different heights for storage flexibility
- Pull-out shelves/bins (some models have these in freezer and fridge)
- Pull-out freezer wire baskets
- Sliding shelves that make cleaning easy and bring items into better view
- Adjustable shelves to store tall items
- A flip-down door/serving tray for access to frequently used items
- See-through drawers
- Separate temperature and humidity controls for meat, fruit, and vegetable compartments
- Sealed storage dishes for leftovers that you can transfer to the microwave oven
- Refreshment centers (where a small self-contained section can be accessed without opening the main door)
- An automatic icemaker (requires a small, 1/4-inch water line that taps into the nearest cold-water line)
- Speed icemaker
- Cold-water, beverage, and ice-cube dispensers on the outside of the refrigerator door, which save energy because you open the door less often.
- Filters for icemakers and water dispensers
- Child lockout (allows disabling of water/ice dispensers, but the icemaker continues to operate)
- A light in the freezer compartment
- Energy Star designation, which means that a refrigerator uses 10 percent less energy than standards allow

Open storage in door

See-through storage on door

Icemaker and water dispenser

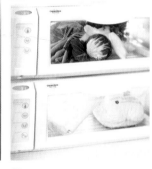

Climate-controlled vegetable and meat bins

Adjustable shelving

Sliding freezer trays

Shelving with hand crank adjustment

Open bin storage for large containers

Cool Coolers

Undercounter Magic

Snack areas with a bar sink, small refrigerator, and separate icemaker offer convenience. Most units are about 24 inches wide and 24 inches deep. But some refrigerators combine with separate icemakers to fit into a standard 30-inch cabinet opening. Most of these units are vented through the front, so they can be almost flush with the cabinets.

Wine coolers store wines at the proper temperatures to maintain perfect flavor. There are many options, including undercounter installation.

above Wine coolers protect fine wines and display them at the same time.

stand-alone FREEZERS

A stand-alone freezer can be a convenient and attractive option—if you've got the space. Some homeowners purchase a separate freezer to place in the garage or basement. The two basic styles are upright or horizontal/chest freezers.

Upright freezers come in manual and self-defrosting models. Convenient to access, self-defrosting uprights look just like refrigerators.

Chest freezers are very efficient and are less expensive. However, it can be difficult to organize and locate items, and all chest freezers have to be manually defrosted. Features to consider when shopping for a freezer:

- Flash defrost, which can speed up the defrosting process on some chest models

- Quick freeze, an option that makes the freezer run continually rather than cycling on and off, and can be handy when adding large amounts of food
- External light to indicate the freezer is working
- Alarm that goes off when the interior of the freezer becomes too warm

Dishwashers

Modern dishwashers are quiet, well-insulated, energy efficient, environmentally friendly, full of features, and easy to use. Most standard dishwashers are loaded from the front and are designed to fit under a standard counter as a built-in appliance. Pre-rinsing is a chore of the past—save time, water, and energy by letting the dishwasher do the dirty work. If you've got the space, 30-inch models are available providing a little extra dishwashing capacity.

Many models have two or three spray arms that hit dishes from several sides and angles with smaller holes in the spray arms that produce a more forceful spray. Spray arms with adjustable water pressure controls (allowing you to reduce the pressure when washing fine china and other delicate items) are worth considering.

Avoid locating your dishwasher near the refrigerator. Also, to help cut down on the noise generated by the dishwasher, consider installing it behind an island or in some other location with built-in noise buffers.

Full of Features

Most models are designed to hold cups, glasses, and other more fragile items on the top rack; plates, pots, and pans, on the bottom rack; and silverware in a special basket. Some models include adjustable racks to make room for larger pots and pans.

Other available features:

- Attachable door panels to match cabinetry
- Display showing time remaining
- Built-in garbage disposers
- Dirt sensors
- Energy-saving drying options
- Rinse and hold cycle
- Pots and pans cycle
- Pause function
- Child lockout, which prevents a cycle from being stopped or interrupted
- Controls located along the top edge of the washer
- Stemware holders
- Delayed starts
- A stainless-steel tub, which resist stains, nicks, and chips and is easy to clean but more expensive than plastic or porcelain-enameled metal finished models

right This front loading dishwasher boasts a stainless-steel tub and heavy-duty wheels on the lower tray.

below Dishwashers are computerized too! Modern dishwashers offer a variety of cycles and control features that focus on specific jobs, from washing fragile glassware to scrubbing dirty pots and pans.

above This built-in dishwasher offers a control panel on top for easy access and has an attached panel that matches the cabinetry.

Ranges

above Advances in technology and design add flexibility and options to modern ranges. Dual fuel, double ovens, sealed cooktops, choices of finish, and sophisticated control functions allow cooks to customize a range to suit their needs.

Whether you call the main cooking appliance a range or a stove, you're referring to a cooking unit that combines an oven and a cooktop. Ranges can be operated with gas, electricity, or a combination of the two. Models are available that can also be fitted for propane.

Effective Use of Space

A range is particularly useful if you have limited space. Ranges, both gas and electric, are available in freestanding and slide-in styles. Add alternative cooking appliances such as a combination microwave-convection oven, an extra wall oven, a warming drawer, or perhaps an extra cooktop in the island.

Range Design Options

Ranges are available to satisfy every kitchen design. You can get the look of a professional kitchen with a stainless-steel commercial-style range, you can add that needed punch with a colorful enamel range, or you may prefer something neutral that will blend in with the cabinetry.

Features to Consider

Whether you are buying a range or separate cooktop and oven units consider these features:

General
- Childproof control locks
- Convection broiling
- Extra oven rack positions
- Larger oven windows
- Electronic and easy-to-read controls and displays
- Delay and time bake cycles
- Heavy-duty oven racks

Electric
- Self-cleaning or continuous-cleaning oven
- Expandable elements (where a smaller heating element is built inside of a larger one, letting you use various size pots efficiently)
- Pan sensor (turns off the element if no pot or pan is on it for more than one minute)
- Hot-surface light indicator
- Variable temperature broiling
- Covered bottom element
- Removable oven floor

Gas
- Continuous grates (double-long grates make it easier to move a pot, but are heavy and harder to clean)
- Automatic reignition

gas or ELECTRIC?

Both gas and electric ranges are efficient and will help you cook a great meal. Professional cooks will often recommend combining a gas cooktop and an electric oven, but the choice is really yours. Here are a few key facts to help you make a decision:

- Gas is less expensive.
- Gas burners don't have to warm up, and with the flame, there is no question that the burner is on.
- An electric cooktop or range is often better for simmering.
- Electric cooktops are efficient and easy to clean.

Electric Ranges

A standard freestanding range is 30 inches wide. Wider sizes and add-on features such as built-in grills and warming drawers are available. Ranges are available in freestanding or slide-in models. Electric ranges require very little maintenance and will last for years.

right A basic electric range has four heating coils. The oven has an element on both top and bottom for baking and broiling. The drawer below offers convenient storage for pots and frying pans.

left Smooth-top electric ranges are a breeze to clean and can be installed to be flush with the countertop to provide extra counter space when not in use. This model boasts a large oven below and a smaller baking oven above. Electronic programming for both ovens frees the cook for other activities.

Gas Ranges

Gas ranges offer precise temperature control for the top burners and quick heating. Gas ranges are usually less expensive to operate than electric models.

below This basic four-burner range offers reliability and style. The drawer below serves as a broiler in a gas oven.

above This professional-style stainless steel gas range offers four high Btu burners and a full convection oven. The commercial look is popular in kitchens.

Cooktops

Electric Cooktops

A cooktop paired with one or more wall ovens offers more flexibility in function and design than does a range. A cooktop fits nicely on an island, and many find the height of a wall oven to be much better for their backs than bending to slide heavy items in and out of a traditional range oven. If you prefer a gas cooktop and an electric oven, having separate units may be more cost-efficient than a dual-fuel range.

Smooth-top cooktops offer several options beyond coils under the surface, including ceramic elements that operate much like traditional coils, halogen elements that heat quickly and glow when they're activated, and induction elements that heat the cookware but not the element itself. Induction cooktops are very expensive and require special cookware.

above Electric cooktops come in several sizes and are available with a smooth top or with traditional coils. Centering the controls in the front eliminates having to reach over hot burners to make adjustments.

right Many cooktops have add-on features including grills, griddles (as shown), and even woks.

Gas Cooktops

Gas cooktops are a popular choice, but remember, if you don't already have gas appliances in your kitchen, you will also have to absorb the expense of hooking up the gas line. Thirty-six-inch models, often in stainless steel, with five or six burners, are growing in popularity.

Pilotless ignition systems are now fairly standard. Smooth-top electric cooktops are easier to clean, but many gas cooktops now come with sealed burners, which reduces cleaning time and makes them more fuel-efficient.

If you go with a larger-than-standard cooktop, make sure you match it up with the appropriate size vent hood. Look for dials that must be pushed in before they can be turned to reduce the chances of accidentally turning on a burner.

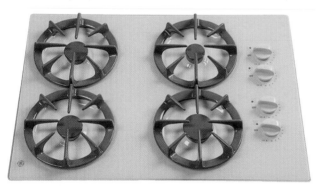

above This gas cooktop makes efficient use of space on a countertop. Controls are placed along the side for easy reach. Sealed burners ease cleaning.

DUAL fuel

If you prefer a gas cooktop and an electric oven, but you don't have room for separate units, then consider one of the many dual-fuel ranges now on the market. Dual-fuel ranges are usually the most expensive in their category but they offer optimum performance for serious cooks.

Ovens

Oven Facts

Standard electric and gas ovens are also referred to as radiant-heat or thermal ovens. They typically have one heating source on the bottom for baking and roasting and a second one on top for broiling.

If you entertain frequently or prepare large meals, you have often faced the challenge of needing to cook two dishes, at different temperatures or by different methods, at the same time. Or if your kitchen is frequently inhabited by two cooks, two ovens can be handy.

Although the general trend is toward larger interior oven space, many wall ovens are not as large as ovens contained within a range. Check the interior and exterior dimensions carefully as you make your plan.

- Buy the most powerful broiler you can afford for better browning.
- Consider variable broiler settings.
- Choose an oven with a large clear window.
- Pick a model with a strong interior light.
- Make sure the racks slide easily.
- Look for features such as delayed start control.

right and above right Double wall ovens create efficient work spaces, but single wall ovens are effective as well. Both are space-savers and add to overall decor.

Convection Ovens

Convection ovens use fans to circulate heated air. These ovens are more energy-efficient and result in faster, more even cooking, producing juicier meats and crustier breads.

Many homeowners today choose a wall oven unit that is a combination conventional and convection oven.

Under the Counter

Undercounter ovens, especially those placed below an island, are a good choice for a second oven when two cooks are at work. While there are special requirements in terms of safety and insulation from heat while cooking, some wall ovens can be mounted below a counter.

Microwaves

Microwave ovens offer convenience and speed. They are the kitchen appliance of choice for teenagers and are appreciated by all of us when heating up leftovers or defrosting meat or vegetables to prepare a quick meal.

Manufacturers continue to improve the technology, but baking and browning are not a microwave's forte.

When a microwave is installed over the cooktop, it is still possible to build a panel-style range hood into the bottom of the microwave.

Some cooks now design for two microwave ovens in their kitchen. One might be placed in the snack area or near the refrigerator. For the cooking center the serious cook may consider a microwave/convection oven combination unit.

Key Features

- Look for models of approximately 1,000 watts
- Turntable
- Steam sensor
- Multiple power levels
- Shortcut controls
- Quick start
- Two-stage cooking
- Convection option

above and below Microwave ovens should be within easy reach of those who intend to use them. Frequent users should purchase a microwave with 1,000 watts of power and 1 to 1.5 cubic feet of cooking space. The ovens are available as built-ins over the range (above) or freestanding (below).

Garbage Disposers

There are two major types of disposals—**continuous feed** and **batch feed**. Many garbage disposals can now be used with septic systems but check local codes to make sure installation is allowed in your location.

- **Continuous-feed** units are activated by a switch on the wall or on the sink. No lid is in place during use.
- **Batch-feed** units operate only when the lid is put in place and partially closed. Having the lid in place lessens the risk of stray utensils being caught in the mechanism.

When selecting a garbage disposal, make sure your sink is strong enough to support the unit. A thin stainless-steel sink may rattle and shake if a garbage disposal unit is installed underneath it.

In-home disposers with motors less than ½ horsepower are not recommended for families with more than two people. One-horsepower units perform more efficiently and effectively, and can handle larger scraps.

Some models are designed to reduce running noise, but there is no such thing as a silent garbage disposer.

Lighting

Ambient Lighting

Ambient lighting is the general lighting that fills the room. During the day, sunlight can provide much of the kitchen's ambient lighting. You also should install adequate ceiling fixtures, track lighting, and/or recessed fixtures. Lighting from ceiling fixtures alone can create unpleasant shadows.

How much light is enough?

A general rule for ambient lighting is 100 watts of incandescent light or 75 watts of fluorescent light per 50 square feet of floor space. You need to consider the height of your ceiling and the color of your walls. Darker colors tend to absorb light, so if your decorating scheme relies on darker tones, you may need additional lighting.

Accent Lighting

Accent lights, used to highlight an interesting architectural feature or artwork, can increase the design impact of your kitchen area. These lights are typically about three times more powerful than general lighting. Low-voltage halogen bulbs are a good choice, as well as a recess downlight with an eyeball lens pointing a beam of light in a particular direction.

The lights in the photo, *below,* are inside the cabinet to highlight its collectibles, as shown *above.*

Task Lighting

Task lighting provides direct light in areas such as above sinks, the food-preparation center, and the cleanup center. Many types of fixtures, including recessed down lights, track lights, hanging pendent lights, and undercabinet strip lights, provide excellent task lighting. It's best to have the lighting for each work center controlled by its own separate wall switch.

How much task light do you need?

Each work center should be illuminated with at least either 100 to 150 watts of incandescent light or 40 to 50 watts of fluorescent light. Strip lighting should be installed under counters. A fluorescent tube should extend along approximately two-thirds of the counter it is illuminating and provide about 8 watts of power per foot of counter space.

bulb BLURBS

- **Incandescent lights** generate a warm glow. They enhance yellow and red hues, are flattering to skin tones, inexpensive, easy to change, and come in a variety of styles.
- **Fluorescent lights** last up to 20 times longer than incandescent and generate up to four times more light as same wattage incandescent bulbs. Fluorescent bulbs now give off a much warmer, softer glow than was available in the past. Some types of fluorescents can be dimmed.

- **Halogen lights** last twice as long as incandescent and are up to three times brighter. Halogen lights radiate all the colors of the spectrum so that the light they produce reflects decorative elements in their true colors. They are small and can be installed in unobtrusive fixtures, such as those popular for undercabinet lighting. These bulbs are more expensive than either incandescent or fluorescent, they burn at high temperatures, are more fragile, and can be damaged if they come into contact with oily substances.

Flooring

More than any other surface, kitchen flooring gets wear and tear. It should be comfortable and durable enough to withstand spills and heavy foot traffic.

Resilient

Resilient flooring describes all synthetic, resin-based flooring and includes vinyl tiles, sheet flooring, linoleum, cork, and rubber.

Vinyl, the most common type of resilient flooring, is inexpensive, flexible, and available in many colors and designs. Some vinyl floors mimic stone and ceramic tiles. Vinyl resists water and stains and is relatively soft.

You can purchase vinyl in sheets or tiles. Vinyl tiles are easier for DIY installation and are less expensive than sheet vinyl.

Linoleum actually becomes more durable the longer it is down. Linoleum costs about twice as much as quality vinyl sheet flooring, but is significantly less expensive than hardwood flooring.

Other choices include **cork** and **rubber**, which are available in muted shades.

Laminate

Laminate flooring comes in planks (which mimic materials like stone and wood) and tiles (which can resemble real tiles or stone). It is strong and durable and resists stains, warping, and scratching. It is quite easy to clean.

Wood

Hardwood, a durable and fairly forgiving surface, is available in many finishes and grain patterns. Most of today's wood floor finishes are suitable for kitchens. The most durable hardwoods are oak, maple, and cherry. Softwoods, such as pine, will dent. However, a distressed pine floor suits a country style. Wood floors require occasional refinishing to remove scratches and stains.

Ceramic Tile and Stone

Ceramic tile is great-looking and easy to clean. This type of flooring has design versatility, as it is available in a myriad of shapes, sizes, textures, and colors. Pattern possibilities are almost limitless.

Stone tiles (marble, limestone, slate, granite) offer a beautiful, natural look. Some stones stain easily, and some are not strong enough to be used for flooring, so choose carefully. The subfloor may need reinforcing to support the weight of the stone. Granite and limestone should be sealed periodically. A low sheen wax or acrylic sealer can be applied to slate.

Carpet

In dry, arid areas of the country, such as the Southwest, low-pile, stain-resistant carpet is often used in kitchens. Non-slip and easy on the feet, carpet is often a good choice for elderly cooks.

Fine Details

You can give your kitchen, dining room, or great-room pizzazz with attention to detail. Express your personal style by accenting the ceiling, floor, or island and displaying artwork and collections in clever ways.

You may think of finishing touches as enhancements that are added once your remodeling project or addition is finished.

After all your hard work, it's fun to choose furnishings and window treatments, and to display artwork, collections, and plants on special shelves and in nooks. Be aware, however, that you need to plan certain details long before the completion date. Architectural elements such as beams, columns, and windows need to be decided in advance.

Decorative accents offer an opportunity to reinforce style. For inspiration review the elements of style in Chapter 1. Also flip through magazines for decorating ideas that will give your kitchen character.

CHAPTER 5 CONTENTS

left Storage baskets displayed on open shelving are both functional and attractive, adding shape and color to the overall design. Paying attention to finishing touches such as hardware, backsplashes, lighting fixtures, trim, and molding on the bases of cabinets and window dressing unifies and completes a successful kitchen scheme.

Ceiling Accents

The beauty of a room does not just surround you. It can cause your gaze to sweep upward. Why just roll a coat of paint on your ceiling? Instead make it a focal point by installing a spectacular chandelier. Wallpaper packs a surprising punch on a ceiling. Install skylights in your kitchen to take advantage of natural light and make a connection with the outside.

left Recessed lighting in the ceiling is used both to accent the molding details on the cabinetry and to provide a warm ambient glow in the kitchen when entertaining. Pleasing use of line and shape is present in the convergence of the cabinetry and columns.

above Line, shape, and color are used effectively to create dynamic geometric patterns. Accentuating existing geometric planes with strong color combinations helps define space and draw focus into the warm, clean colors in the kitchen area.

left Skylights and accent lighting hidden behind crown molding balance the height of this dining room's tray ceiling and create dramatic contrast both day and night. The strong architectural lines are reinforced by the simplicity of the chandelier.

SUSPENDED
beauty

An appropriately sized chandelier is an inch long for every foot of room length. Avoid mounting the fixture too high. In a room with an 8-foot ceiling, it should hang 25 to 30 inches above the table. For each foot higher than 8 feet, raise the chandelier to maintain proportion in the room. Install a dimmer switch, too, so you can adjust the mood depending on the occasion.

Columns

Columns have a decorative purpose, even when they do not hold up a wall. They define areas within large spaces. Columns stylishly divide large kitchens from great-rooms or dining areas. If you use this architectural element to break up space, match it to your decorating style.

far right This column provides separation between the cooking area and the room beyond. It also draws the eye to the coffered ceiling above.

right This column's ornate base creates a dynamic juxtaposition to the simple lines of the raised counter on which it rests. Columns offer a sense of stability in a room.

Art Underfoot

Rugs add color and texture to a room. Like a fine painting they can serve as a focal point. If your kitchen or dining area seems dull, design your own tile rug. But think carefully before you put down the tile. This type of floor accent is not easily removed.

left A rug of primary tiles sets off this rough-hewn island. Mixing contrasting materials represents a bold expression of personal style.

above An intricate grid of diamond and square shapes marks the floor of this dining room. Against the soft gray and blush surface, the blue and black tiles make a striking border.

Island Brackets

An island should be practical, with attention to such concerns as electrical outlets placed on the side, adequate knee space, and edges that are rounded or beveled. It is also like a piece of furniture, which needs to coordinate with the kitchen's overall decorating scheme. If installing an island, make sure it has stylish details, from the choice of countertop material to the toe-kick at the base. Adding brackets to these islands adds structural interest and charm.

below A complex and ornate carved bracket such as the one shown here complements old-world styles such as Tuscan or Mediterranean.

left This hickory bracket undulates in contrast to the straight, narrow lines of the hickory beaded board. A fussy bracket would not tie in with the solid, dependable look of this island.

right Subtly scalloped brackets lend curves amid the lines of a streamlined country kitchen. Such detail creates the impression of a table, inviting family members to pull up stools.

Shelf Life

Use shelves as a way to store cookbooks and showcase collectibles. If you need a starting point for arranging collections, try grouping items by type, color, or pattern. To keep the eye moving, vary heights of objects.

right Open shelving at the end of corner cabinets offers space to display collections. Here fine glassware takes center stage and adds contrasting color accents to the lightness of the blond cabinetry.

above Elevate utilitarian objects, such as canisters and clear jars filled with different colored pasta and pickled peppers, to the level of art by placing them in open shelving. This set of contemporary shelves is actually a workshop project. They're made from lengths of 1×8 pine. The boxes can be painted the same color as the walls, or try different color combinations for a more striking look.

above In the dining area of this country kitchen, a galley shelf displays collectibles, drawing the eye upward. The warm wood of the crown molding, shelf, and chair rail brings unity, while the staggered heights of objects creates variety.

above Integrated accessories such as this shelf and paper towel holder make use of the space between wall and base cabinets. Note the built-in wine rack.

Frame a View

Light streaming through windows makes your kitchen a pleasant place in which to cook and spend time with your family. Dress your windows up or down in keeping with the room's dominant style.

above This dining area takes advantage of an unusual corner window that creates a wraparound view.

above Large open windows offer the cook a view of the cityscape in this downtown loft kitchen.

right Well-insulated oversize sliding doors bring the outdoors into this kitchen no matter what the season.

More Than Just a Floor

The floor is sometimes referred to as the fifth wall because you must pay as much attention to what covers it as you would for the walls themselves. The right flooring provides comfort and safety, functions as a unifying design element, and creates successful transitions between rooms. Consider mixing textures and color to create unique patterns and combinations.

below Flooring in kitchens should be safe to walk on, easy to maintain, and resistant to damage from water and food spills.

Splash Walls With Color

Incorporating art into your kitchen does not require investing in expensive paintings. Browse flea markets for vintage still life and landscape paintings. Reproduction botanical prints and large museum posters with dynamic colors are also striking. To preserve photographs and artwork of value, have them professionally mounted and framed with acid-free materials.

above An inexpensive framed poster adds color and flair.

above The orange in this painting is the complementary color to the blue trim and television cabinet below.

above The print, which is relatively neutral in tone, draws focus because of the dark frame.

PRODUCTIVE arrangement

You may be eager to fill your walls with art, but be patient when hanging pictures. Experiment first. Cut out pieces of paper the size and shape of photographs and artwork, arrange them on the floor, then tape them up. (Use low-tack blue masking tape so newly painted walls will stay fresh.) Arrange them in rows or in a circle. Larger and darker artwork usually looks best when placed at the bottom of an arrangement. To keep an arrangement from appearing static, vary pictures that have similar colors. If you have an especially large grouping, lay it out on the floor first. Getting a bird's-eye view, you can move pictures around quickly as you figure out a preliminary arrangement. If the work is particularly heavy, drive hangers directly into studs.

Knobs, Handles, Hinges, and Pulls

If great designs are in the details, then choosing the right hardware to complement beautiful cabinetry is one of the most important decisions you will make. Home centers and cabinet shops offer hundreds of options to provide the perfect finishing touch to any kitchen.

right Whatever the material, handles must be easy to grasp and securely mounted to the cabinet doors. Bring home samples so you can make informed choices about style and color.

left Mounting handles and pulls requires precise measuring. Templates for centering and height guarantee consistency of installation.

right Knobs require only a single hole for mounting and are less obtrusive than handles or pulls. All face-mounted cabinet hardware provides both repetition and visual movement in a kitchen.

left Some hinges, such as the hand-forged example on the far left, make bold design statements. The barrel hinge in the center adds a simple accent. Frameless cabinetry relies on hidden hinges such as the one on the near left.

Lighting is a Key

Lighting is a major factor in creating a relaxing and comforting ambience in a kitchen. As with most of the elements that make up a kitchen, lighting serves both a practical and aesthetic function. Whether natural or ambient, lighting as a design element creates mood and focus. Proper lighting is also essential for safety and for making the kitchen efficient and easy to use.

above Recessed lighting in the soffit creates dramatic shadowing and accents the sleek architectural lines of the cabinetry.

above This Arts and Crafts light fixture provides illumination and instantly identifies the style of this room.

above High-quality reproductions of old lighting fixtures offer a less expensive alternative to refurbished antiques.

Go with the Flow

To many people faucets are the jewels of the kitchen, and no wonder. They are available in hundreds of models, configurations, and materials to suit any design requirement. Since you've got to wash your lettuce anyway, you might as well do it in style.

above and right Match the finish and style of your faucets to the overall style of the room. It's equally important to consider function, ease of maintenance, and accessibility of parts as you make your decisions.

Universal Design

Universal design makes this kitchen and great-room efficient, accessible, and comfortable for all, without sacrificing style.

The beauty of universal design is its intent to make housing usable by everyone through all of life's stages and changes. If you're in the early planning stages of building or renovating a house, incorporating universal design is a wise long-term investment.

In most cases you won't need to make significant changes whatever the circumstances: a family member becoming permanently or temporarily disabled, an elderly parent in the home, a young child or a shorter-than-average adult, or guests with disabilities. Free of obstacles, your home will be enjoyable for all. And if you're planning to live there for many years, universal design features will accommodate your own needs in the future, whether you sprain a wrist, develop stiff joints, or need assistance to move about.

CHAPTER 6 CONTENTS

left Craftsman style beautifully translates to the open, friendly interior of this convenient 21st-century kitchen and great-room.

Smart Design for Everyone

Universal design is now mainstream because of growing awareness and changes in population demographics. As baby boomers enter their 50s and 60s, many will be building or remodeling homes for when they retire. Universal design will serve them well in preparing a comfortable, safe environment for their later years.

Successful implementation of universal design does not produce a sterile, institutional look. Instead it results in a functional and attractive setting where your family and friends can savor their surroundings, drawn by a pleasing combination of colors, textures, and surfaces that is heightened by engaging finishing touches.

Universal design can be affordable. The 1,300-square-foot house highlighted in this chapter cost $130,000 to build with all materials as stock. Universal design features and products are almost undetectable and increase expenses no more than 3 percent if implemented as part of the original design.

With particular attention to placement, shape, and size, universal design features make the house easier for all family members and visitors, regardless of physical ability. For instance, if you put light switches and electrical outlets between 44 and 48 inches from the floor, anyone who has trouble bending over or reaching up will not struggle to plug in an appliance or turn on a light.

The shape of something as simple as a doorknob affects how easily someone can enter and leave a room. Comparably priced lever-style door handles are easier to turn than knobs and are available in a range of styles and finishes. Anyone experiencing arthritis will appreciate the action, which is easy on the wrist.

Making halls a little wider and installing doors at least 32 inches wide is convenient for everyone. Wider doorways are a must for wheelchair users or those who use walkers, but spacious doorways also make movement throughout the home easier. For instance, a 36-inch-wide door simplifies tasks such as moving furniture in or out of the house or between rooms and lessens the likelihood of damaging walls and doorjambs.

An entrance based on universal design eliminates steps, simplifying coming and going, especially if you're carrying in groceries, rolling a suitcase, pushing a baby stroller, or guiding a wheelchair. When bad weather causes wet or icy conditions, more secure footing lessens the worry about slipping on the walkway.

To ensure safety and usability for anyone entering or leaving the house, follow these guidelines:

- Plan for at least one level entrance with no steps into your home, eliminating raised sills on the exterior door.
- Ensure a flush threshold, with a maximum of ½-inch rise.
- Use a beveled strip at the bottom door track of sliding glass doors to prevent tripping.
- Install a sidelight by the entrance door or dual peep holes with one 42 to 48 inches high.
- Locate address numbers so they are visible from the street.

left Wide spacing around the island allows anyone in a wheelchair to easily maneuver from one workstation to another. Universal design guidelines recommend that traffic lanes be at least 3 feet wide, preferably wider, and at least 5 feet in diameter in places where a wheelchair user needs to maneuver.

left Plenty of light through skylights, wide windows, and doors makes the kitchen and great-room a warm, welcoming space. The casement windows open with a crank, which could be motorized, allowing people of all ages and capabilities to operate them. Two zero-step entrances allow easy access, a plus for anyone carrying bags of groceries or pushing a baby stroller or a wheelchair. Doors based on universal design are at least 3 feet wide. Lever-style handles take little effort to operate.

- Make sure walkways have a gentle slope of no more than 5 percent.
- Provide an accessible route with no steps from parking or vehicle drop-off.
- Light the exterior of the entry door with motion sensor lights.
- Cover the entryway for protection from weather, and provide a safe place to wait.
- Allow a space of at least 18 inches on the latch side of the door.
- Push-button combination locks are easier to use than keys.
- Exterior doors should be at least 36 inches wide and interior doors 32 inches.
- Ensure that no more than 5 pounds of force is needed to open doors.
- Replace standard hinges with swing-free hinges to increase the door opening.
- Have a bench or package shelf available beside the door to hold items you may bring in from the car.
- Make circulation paths at least 3 feet wide.
- Consider using pocket doors for the interior when hall and room space is limited.
- Fit interior doorways with lever-style door handles.
- Move all objects and furniture that can obstruct passages.
- Install handrails at exterior steps for safer travel up and down.

mainstreaming
UNIVERSAL DESIGN

The seven basic principles of universal design:

- **Equitable Use:** Making the design useful and marketable to people with diverse abilities.
- **Flexibility in Use:** Accommodating the many differences in individual preferences and abilities.
- **Simple and Intuitive Use:** Making the design easy to understand, regardless of the user's experience, knowledge, language skills, or current concentration level.
- **Perceptible Information:** Communicating information effectively to the user, regardless of the ambient conditions or the user's sensory abilities.
- **Tolerance for Error:** Minimizing hazards and adverse consequences of accidental or unintended actions.
- **Low Physical Effort:** Making the design easy and comfortable with minimum fatigue.
- **Size and Space for Approach and Use:** Providing appropriate size and space for approach, reach, manipulation, and use, regardless of user's body size, posture, or mobility.

Food-Prep Convenience

The L-shape kitchen's work triangle minimizes unnecessary trips and reduces fatigue. Open space makes fixtures, appliances, and workstations easy to reach and use by most cooks. The sink and other work spaces are located within universal reach range, which means the cook, if seated, does not have to lean and strain to turn on the faucet or pick up a heavy item from a high countertop. Keeping a basic set of cooking utensils at every workstation also saves steps. These guidelines also make the food-prep area more usable:

- If you install two sinks, mount them at two heights, with the edge of the highest no more than 34 inches.

- At least one sink should provide clear knee space that measures at least 27 inches high, 30 inches wide, and 19 inches deep. (Wider is better.)
- Sink basins should be no more than 6½ inches deep with a rear drain for people who prefer to sit or to allow children to use a step stool.
- Insulate the bottom of the sink and the water pipes to protect any seated cook from burns and/or cuts.
- Make sure fixtures and other workstations are within universal reach range (15 to 48 inches).
- Install single-handle/lever faucets that can be operated with a closed fist.
- Choose a sprayer with an extra long hose.
- Place the sink near the range so you can use the sprayer to fill pots while on the burner.
- Consider a garbage disposer at a double-basin sink provided kneespace can be made under one sink.

left The pullout towel rack is readily accessible.

below The single-lever faucet requires only one hand to operate. The sprayer is also easy to grab.

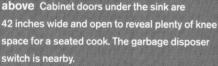

above Cabinet doors under the sink are 42 inches wide and open to reveal plenty of knee space for a seated cook. The garbage disposer switch is nearby.

right Beauty was not spared on the island, as this monochromatic tile pattern shows. The island countertop, where company is most likely to sit, is made of solid-surfacing. Less expensive laminate is used on the other countertops.

above The Craftsman-style pendant, made of formica and metal, directs light over the sink while casting a glow throughout the kitchen.

Efficient Storage

Although this house is not large, every inch of space is used. A pullout pantry and pull-down shelves put items at the fingertips of short or seated cooks. Universally designed storage offers great options for all homeowners. Follow these guidelines:

- Vary cabinet sizes for use by family members of different heights and physical needs; consider children and tall men or women.
- Use lowered wall cabinets or pull-down storage units so objects and supplies are within the universal reach range requirements of 15 to 48 inches.
- Include cabinets that allow for knee space (at least 27 inches high, 30 inches wide, and 19 inches deep).
- Consider cabinet doors that slide back into the cabinet.
- Place magnetic latches on cabinets for easier closure.

- Choose cabinet components that facilitate access to stored supplies and appliances, including larger, heavier items: rotating units, such as lazy Susans; shelves that pull or roll out of base cabinets; and full-extension drawers.
- Use a wide entry and storage units that rotate or pull out for a walk-in pantry.
- Install pull-out shelves in base cabinets.
- Consider loop handles on cabinet doors and drawers.
- Use shelves that are height adjustable in wall cabinets or are just above countertops.
- Install shelves that move up and down for maximum storage in full-height pantries.
- Consider shelves 4 to 6 inches wide at the back of the counter for convenient everyday storage.

left These pullout pantry shelves, which are shown pulled out, make nonperishable items easy to reach.

above A pullout work surface can be used for rolling out dough, chopping vegetables, or working on school assignments or family craft projects.

cold **STORAGE**

The homeowners placed the refrigerator and pantry close together to aid in food preparation and unloading groceries.

- Side-by-side refrigerators offer access at a variety of heights usable by everyone.
- Icemakers and water dispensers in the refrigerator door are convenient for everyone.
- The refrigerator/freezer is on a raised platform.
- Roll-out drawers ease access to food.
- Spill-proof shelves, container storage in the door, slide-out shelves, and see-through vegetable bins ease access.
- Door handles require minimal effort and finger use.

below A pullout mesh basket keeps onions and potatoes fresh.

Cooking Center

Safety and comfort are paramount for anyone who cooks. Oven controls should be easy to read and require little gripping to turn. Instead of the coil burners shown here, some homeowners prefer smooth glass tops so they can slide heavy pots and pans to the countertop. However, smooth glass cooktops are not good for people with low vision or who are blind. Here are other considerations when shopping for a range.

■ An indicator light on the range that warns if a burner is hot helps prevent burns.

■ You won't need an overhead vent hood if you install a downdraft venting system, which has vents at the center or at the back of the cooktop. They are equipped with high-power fans that pull heat away from the user.

■ Alarms on the range must be both visual and audible.

■ Allow sufficient room on both sides of the oven for easier access to the oven interior.

■ Self-cleaning ovens are good timesavers.

■ Place the microwave oven at counter height with a pull-out shelf in front and knee space below.

above Readable graphics—white pops out on a black or gray surface—and easily turned knobs make cooking easier and safer. Having the controls at the front of the oven also prevents a seated cook from reaching over hot burners.

above High-illumination lighting sources are important to cooks, allowing them to see clearly.

above This hammered brushed-nickel pull is good looking and easy to grasp.

left Pots and pans slide out next to the stove.

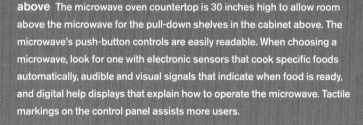

above and below Behind conventional pantry doors is a handy pull-down shelf.

above The microwave oven countertop is 30 inches high to allow room above the microwave for the pull-down shelves in the cabinet above. The microwave's push-button controls are easily readable. When choosing a microwave, look for one with electronic sensors that cook specific foods automatically, audible and visual signals that indicate when food is ready, and digital help displays that explain how to operate the microwave. Tactile markings on the control panel assists more users.

Countertops should have rounded edges and corners. There is plenty of counter space beside the cooktop and oven, easing removal of hot pots. These guidelines make countertops functional:

- Use a contrasting color for the border treatment on countertops to enhance visibility.
- Install fold-down shelves or pull-out countertops to meet all family members' size requirements.
- Install easy-clean surfaces.
- Have continuous countertop space to slide heavy objects.
- Plan a food-preparation countertop that is 30 to 32 inches high with knee space below.
- Install a pull-out cutting board 30 inches high below the countertop.
- Install heatproof surfaces, especially near cooking appliances.
- A slightly lipped countertop edge minimizes spills running off onto the floor.

above A quick turn of the lazy Susan in the corner cabinet makes contents visible at first glance and handy at first reach.

Kitchen Design and Planning **165**

People-Friendly Cleanup Center

Washing dishes or clothes may not be the high point of your day, however, installation of a raised dishwasher and convenient laundry center make these chores easier.

Raising the height of the washer and dryer also helps you avoid excess bending. You can effortlessly toss clothes into a front-loading washer, which uses less detergent, and a front-loading dryer. The tops of both come in handy as counter space. Make sure the lint catcher is in front for easier cleaning.

Extend convenience into your closets. Install adjustable-height shelving (great for growing kids) and hang clothing on a motorized clothing carousel. Double racks in closets allow for less reach and more storage space.

above The raised dishwasher tucks into the island alongside the sink, which makes rinsing and loading dishes a breeze.

right Installing a dishwasher at a raised height reduces extra bending, stooping, or reaching.

Dishwasher

Raise the height of the dishwasher 6 to 16 inches to eliminate extra bending.

Look for a dishwasher with these features: controls on the upper rim of the door; automatic soil-content, water-temperature, and cycle-selection sensors; flexible loading features such as fold-down tines; a lockout switch to prevent accidental operation; an easy-to-read display; and electronic problem indicators. A dishwasher drawer unit is another option, especially for a household of one or two people. Also consider high contrast lettering indicating function, and large buttons (smooth control areas are difficult for people with low vision).

above Bifold doors hide the laundry center from the kitchen.

right Extra storage is available to the right of the dryer.

above The raised front-loading washer and dryer, like the dishwasher, reduce extra bending and stooping. Controls at the front make appliances accessible for a person using a wheelchair and more comfortable for all users.

no-slip
FLOORS

This house uses matte ceramic tile and carpeting to prevent slipping. Here are some other ways to keep traffic moving smoothly through your home:

- Install level nonskid flooring (prefinished hardwood is a good choice).
- Choose surfaces such as vinyl, wood, and low-pile carpeting, which do not impede the movement of wheels.
- Use different flooring for tactile clues for navigation, such as tile in the entrance, carpet in the living room, and vinyl in the kitchen.
- Secure the edges of area rugs.
- Remove throw or scatter rugs to minimize tripping.
- Install lighting at floor level and along stairs to enhance vision.
- Leave a clear, unobstructed 30×48-inch floor space in front of the refrigerator, range, microwave, sink, countertops, and dishwasher.
- Leave a minimum of 60 inches in diameter in the kitchen to allow a wheelchair to turn 360 degrees.

LET THERE
BE light

- To reduce bending, place electrical outlets 18 to 24 inches above the floor.
- Motion-sensitive lighting or touch lights are easier for everyone to use and especially helpful when a family member lacks dexterity.
- Light switches should be mounted 44 to 48 inches above the floor.
- Light switches that slide up and down are easier to turn on and off.
- Glowing light switches can be seen in the dark.
- Provide ambient lighting for overall room illumination, task lighting over work areas, and accent lighting to focus on art and objects.
- Reduce glare with window treatments, textured wallpaper, matte wall paint, or low-gloss floors.

BEFORE

Remodeling Diary

This basic remodeling, which was completed between early February and mid-April, resulted in a welcoming space for John and Lisa Egan.

This case study leads you through the real-life experience of John and Lisa Egan as they remodel their kitchen. The couple went through the seven stages common to remodeling projects: Planning, Demolition, Roughing-In the Space, Priming and Painting, Cabinets, Countertops, and Finishing Up.

The story begins with the homeowners' dreams, ideas, and priorities, followed by concrete planning. You will see their initial ideas, how they implemented the planning process suggested in Chapter 3, and look at the budgeting process and trade-offs the homeowners made. For John and Lisa, the planning phase lasted approximately four weeks, and products took one to two weeks to arrive. Installation took almost five weeks and involved 19 actual work days at the Egan home. A timeline running along the bottom of the pages in this chapter reveals a start-to-finish overview of the remodeling diary. The chronology begins on page 170.

CHAPTER 7 CONTENTS

left This project fell within the price range of an average kitchen makeover. The remodeling process is one of problem solving and decision making. It takes proper planning and attention to details to realize a beautiful and functional kitchen from the modest beginnings.

Planning

Budget Boundaries

A wisely planned and executed kitchen remodel allows a homeowner to recoup about 70–80 percent of the cost when the house is sold. A cosmetic facelift may cost several thousand dollars. A complete remodeling ranges from $12,000 to $75,000 or more. The lower end of the scale is usually between $12,000 to $20,000. Changes typically include new stock cabinets, countertops, sinks, fixtures, flooring, lighting, and basic-model appliances. The average cost of a complete kitchen remodeling is about $36,000, according to the National Kitchen and Bath Association. Expenses go up if a homeowner reconfigures a kitchen and incorporates custom cabinetry and commercial-grade appliances.

Generally the budget should not exceed 15 percent of a home's total value. John and Lisa crunched numbers and decided they wanted to stay under $24,000. In the end they succeeded, coming in at $22,800. Here's how it happened.

Week 1: Assessment of Existing Kitchen

The Egans assess their existing kitchen. Early discussions revealed two key factors: Their budget did not allow for an expansion, and they wanted to keep their wood floor. This planning led to the decision to keep the same basic footprint, an L-shape with a peninsula, with some minor adjustments.

After reviewing their initial wish list, the couple set their priorities:

- New cabinets and countertops to increase their storage space
- A new sink and faucet
- New appliances
- Improved lighting, including new fixtures
- A decorative paint finish
- A new door leading to the patio
- New window treatments

They measured the existing space before meeting with a kitchen and bath design professional. These homeowners developed an outline of a plan and budget. Early on they opted to hire professionals to complete the job rather than doing the work themselves. After considering the various types of professionals and the extent of the remodeling job, they decided to work with a general contractor and a certified kitchen and bath designer at a home center.

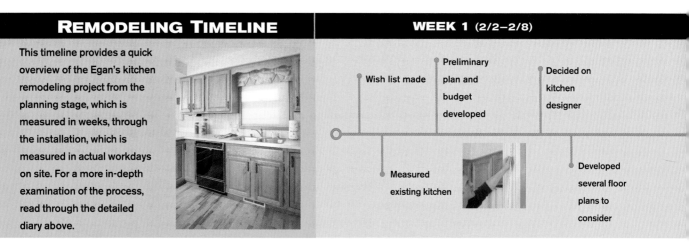

REMODELING TIMELINE

This timeline provides a quick overview of the Egan's kitchen remodeling project from the planning stage, which is measured in weeks, through the installation, which is measured in actual workdays on site. For a more in-depth examination of the process, read through the detailed diary above.

WEEK 1 (2/2–2/8)

Wish list made

Preliminary plan and budget developed

Decided on kitchen designer

Measured existing kitchen

Developed several floor plans to consider

Week 2: Working With a Designer

In their first meeting with kitchen designer Beth Loerke, John and Lisa developed a floor plan with options. During this process they decided that although they would purchase new appliances, they would not change the location of the sink or the stove. Working with different floor plans revealed that moving the refrigerator would help them achieve a goal of maximizing storage space. They agreed that tearing out an existing closet and moving the refrigerator would be the only changes to the footprint of the existing kitchen.

Understanding that storage was a key factor, and given that a large percentage of many remodeling budgets is often allocated to cabinetry, Beth suggested the couple continue their research before their next planning meeting. She also suggested the couple revisit the assessment of their current kitchen and their wish lists. The focus was on storage space: how they use it, where items are kept, and how John and Lisa envision using their new cabinet space.

Budget Trade-Off

After reassessing their needs and reviewing cabinet options and costs, the Egans realized that their budget would not allow for a solid-surfacing countertop. They opted for a less-expensive laminate countertop in order to keep all the storage they wanted.

"When people are tackling a remodeling project, I like to encourage them to review the existing space and develop a list of likes and dislikes, then prioritize what they want. I like to have people determine a budget because then you can start reviewing options for materials. Then you can draw up plans and spend some time with them."

—Beth Loerke, Kitchen Designer

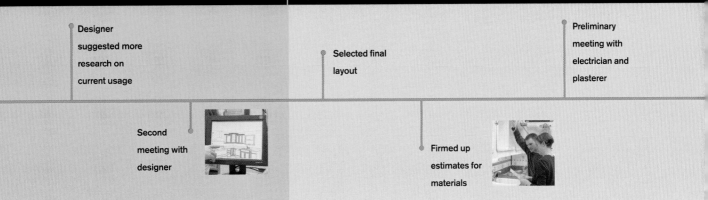

WEEK 2 (2/9–2/15)	**WEEK 3 (2/16–2/22)**
Designer suggested more research on current usage	Preliminary meeting with electrician and plasterer
	Selected final layout
Second meeting with designer	Firmed up estimates for materials

Weeks 3–4: Finalizing the Plan

The Egans met again with their kitchen designer to select a final layout and get firm cost estimates for some of the materials. They selected cabinets, countertops, backsplash tiles, cabinetry hardware, and paint colors.

John and Lisa began deeper planning by meeting with the electrician and plasterers. Although these professionals were able to provide some useful suggestions, they were not able to provide accurate quotes because many details in the remodeling plan had not yet been finalized. The Egans also met with a painter to get a bid for painting the walls, which included costs for a decorative finish, and the ceiling.

The Egans started shopping for light fixtures, appliances, sinks and faucets, window treatments, and new dining chairs for the peninsula seating.

right and above right
John and Lisa take the designer's advice to spend time looking over their options and finalizing their design to meet their needs.

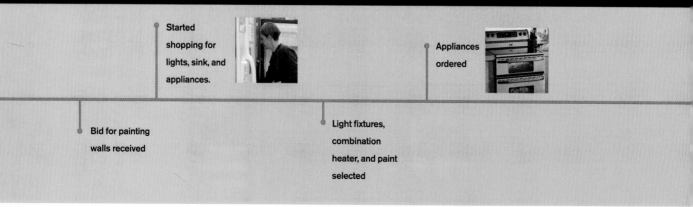

WEEK 4 (2/23–3/1)

Started shopping for lights, sink, and appliances.

Appliances ordered

Bid for painting walls received

Light fixtures, combination heater, and paint selected

The homeowners made decisions with confidence because they did not rush the process. By the end of week 4, they had:

■ Selected their appliances and placed the order

■ Made their final decisions about painting and plastering

■ Selected the tile backsplash

■ Consulted with the electrician and decided to place recessed lights in the main area of the kitchen

■ Chosen the light fixture for the dining area and picked out the window treatments

right John and Lisa browse the aisles of their local home center researching features they want in appliances for their kitchen.

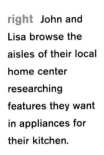

Expect the Unexpected

Every renovation project offers its share of surprises. The Egans initially planned to tear out an existing closet in the kitchen, which was being used as a pantry. They consulted with their general contractor to help them analyze their options.

Getting the contractor's input in the planning phase proved to be a wise decision. Ripping out the closet presented a couple of problems. Contractor Rick Nadke explained that the closet contained attic access and that building codes require first-floor access to the attic. The problem was solved by moving access to a front hall closet. A second problem was that one of the closet walls was a load-bearing wall next to a chimney.

Ripping this out would have required installing a new hot water heater, capping off the chimney, and shoring up the structure to replace the load-bearing wall. All in all it was better to leave the wall in place.

WEEK 5 (3/2–3/8)

Decided to use recessed lights

Tile for backsplash selected

Light fixture for dining area chosen

Demolition

Workdays 1–3

Removing a wall cabinet.

Workday 1

Demolition is a job many homeowners choose to do themselves to save money, but in this case the entire project was handled by contractors. The Egans were replacing the cabinets, countertops, and appliances. The existing floor needed to be protected with cardboard that extended into the living room area. The refrigerator was moved into the living room, and they created a temporary kitchen with a microwave oven in the family room.

Demolition began with the removal of the appliances, the wall cabinets, and the countertops. This left clear space to tear down the closet wall and soffit.

Prying up a countertop.

Removing the countertop.

be **CAREFUL**

If you're doing the demolition yourself, be sure to wear proper safety gear, including heavy gloves, eye protection, and a dust respirator. Work carefully when tearing down walls. An electrical wire or plumbing pipe may be lurking back there.

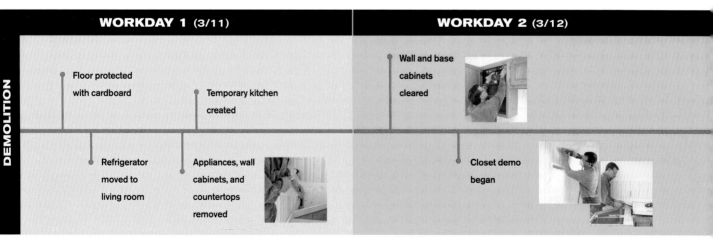

DEMOLITION

WORKDAY 1 (3/11)

- Floor protected with cardboard
- Temporary kitchen created
- Refrigerator moved to living room
- Appliances, wall cabinets, and countertops removed

WORKDAY 2 (3/12)

- Wall and base cabinets cleared
- Closet demo began

Workday 2

Once the wall and base cabinets were cleared (with the exception of the sink cabinet, which remained as a water source) workers began removing the closet. Nails were cut across the top with a reciprocating saw and drywall was removed to expose the studs. The next step was to remove the header and then the soffit enclosure next to the closet.

Workday 3

Removing the lighting soffit that was mounted above the old peninsula marked the end of general demolition. Once the soffit was down, a scrap of drywall was screwed into place as a patch. Eventually blueboard was installed on the ceiling. The homeowners decided on a plaster skim coat as a base for a decorative faux finish on the walls and a textured swirl pattern for on the ceiling.

Removing the wallpaper and roughing-in the electrical system to prepare the walls and ceiling for the backerboard came next. Removing wallpaper is never an easy job, and this case proved no exception. It took two full days to remove all the paper.

Cutting through nails holding the stud wall to the ceiling.

Demolishing the closet wall.

Removing the closet header.

Removing the closet soffit.

Removing the soffit above the peninsula.

Filling the soffit hole with drywall.

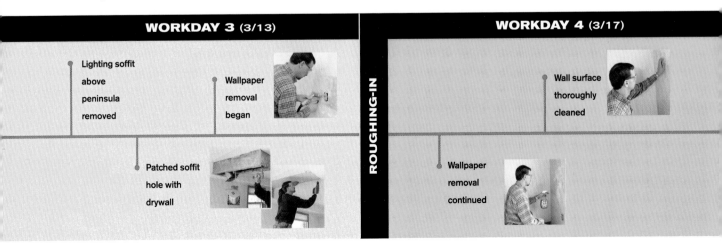

WORKDAY 3 (3/13)

Lighting soffit above peninsula removed

Wallpaper removal began

Patched soffit hole with drywall

WORKDAY 4 (3/17)

ROUGHING-IN

Wall surface thoroughly cleaned

Wallpaper removal continued

Roughing-In the Space
Workdays 4–10

Workdays 4–5

Once wallpaper is removed, the job is only half over. The surface must be thoroughly cleaned to remove any glue residue. All dings, cracks, and gouges must then be carefully repaired. A steamer and putty knife are often required to get the job done properly.

"We discovered that the wallpaper in the house was not properly sized when it was hung, which made removal really difficult. We tried everything. Eventually we found that a combination of a gel remover, a wallpaper scorer, and a steamer did the trick, but it took a lot longer than we thought it would."

—*Lisa Egan, Homeowner*

Workday 6

After the wallpaper was removed, the electricians came to rough-in the wiring for the recessed lighting. They completed the work at this point so the lights would be ready to install when the new ceiling was in place.

"Our electrician recommended recessed lighting, which allowed for better coverage, fewer shadows, and a cleaner, open feel. I wasn't 100 percent sold on the idea because I hadn't liked the lighting in our old soffits, but decided to follow his advice."

—*John Egan, Homeowner*

Workday 7

The sink and final cabinetry were removed and the access panel to the attic, required by code, was moved into the closet in the living room.

Moving the access panel had become an important part of the overall project.

Cleaning wallpaper paste from the wall.

Repairing damage to the drywall.

Running cable for a recessed fixture.

Feeding wire from the attic for the recessed fixtures.

Disconnecting the sink to remove the final cabinet.

Framing out the access panel in the living room closet.

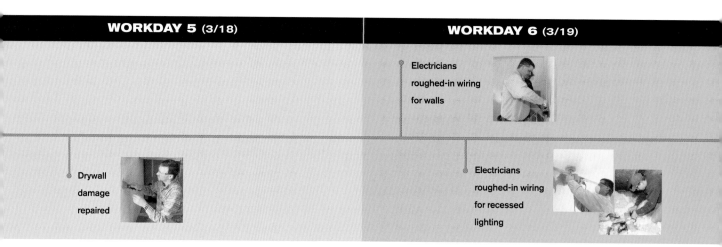

WORKDAY 5 (3/18)

Drywall damage repaired

WORKDAY 6 (3/19)

Electricians roughed-in wiring for walls

Electricians roughed-in wiring for recessed lighting

"Code required us to have a first-floor access to the attic, and if we were not able to create a new one, we would not have been able to convert the kitchen closet into functional storage like we did."

—John Egan, Homeowner

Since the sink and stove remained in their locations, plumbing and gas line considerations were minimal. The only exception was running a water line for the icemaker in the new refrigerator. If the layout is satisfactory, reinstalling new appliances in the old locations is cost-effective and saves a great deal of time.

Workday 8

One of the messiest parts of the project involved removing the popcorn ceiling to install the blueboard required for the plaster treatment on the ceilings and walls. Scraping popcorn off a ceiling is a difficult and dusty job.

Once the ceiling was clean, the plasterers began their work. A bonding agent had to be applied to all surfaces before plastering. While the team hung the backerboard on the ceiling using a combination of ladders and stilts, the bonding agent was applied to the walls. Cuts were made for the recessed lighting as they went. The walls were plastered while the joint compound and tape was drying on the ceiling. After the bonding agent was applied to the ceiling, it was given its plaster coat. The plaster coats on the walls and ceiling provide a solid base for the faux finish that is to come.

necessary PERMITS

Because no plumbing was moved, a plumbing permit was not required, but a licensed plumber hooked up the icemaker and the dishwasher. The electrical work required a permit and there was an inspection prior to sealing the walls and finishing the installation of the fixtures. It's essential that you meet local code requirements and have the necessary inspections along the way.

Scraping popcorn off the ceiling.

Hanging blueboard on the ceiling.

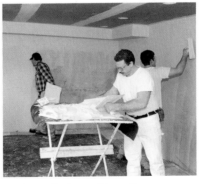

Applying plaster coat to walls.

Applying plaster coat to ceiling.

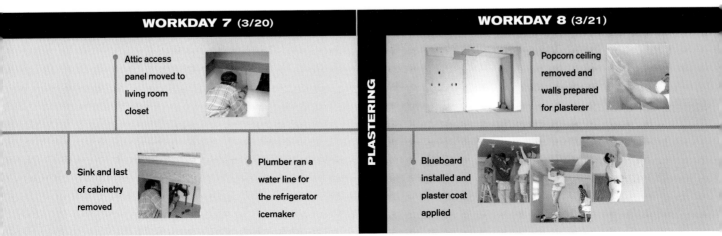

WORKDAY 7 (3/20)

- Attic access panel moved to living room closet
- Sink and last of cabinetry removed
- Plumber ran a water line for the refrigerator icemaker

PLASTERING

WORKDAY 8 (3/21)

- Popcorn ceiling removed and walls prepared for plasterer
- Blueboard installed and plaster coat applied

Workday 9

Over the course of Day 9, the plaster work was completed. The walls and ceiling were sand-floated to match adjoining areas, and a broader fanning technique was used on the ceiling.

Plastering is messy, and the next step was to prime the walls in preparation for the faux painting technique to come, so cleanup had to be thorough to ensure the walls and ceiling were free of dust and debris.

Skimming on the first plaster coat.

Floating the plaster to smooth it.

cleanup **MATTERS**

Reliable contractors pick up after themselves every day, and do major cleaning between work segments. This is especially important when the remodeling project moves from the demolition and prep phases to painting, installation, and adding the finishing touches.

Skimming on the final plaster coat.

Floating the plaster to create a slight texture on the ceiling and soffits.

Cleanup in preparation for priming and painting.

WORKDAY 9 (3/24)

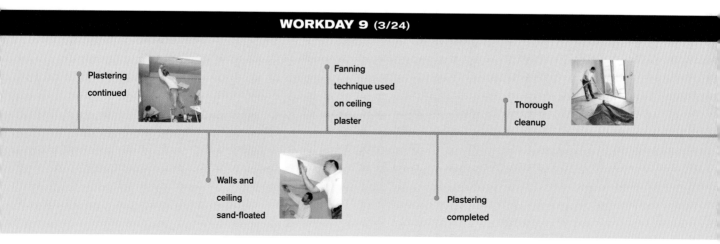

Plastering continued

Fanning technique used on ceiling plaster

Thorough cleanup

Walls and ceiling sand-floated

Plastering completed

Priming and Painting
Workdays 10–11

Workday 10

On Day 10 the painter began to prime the freshly plastered walls and ceiling. Primer is specially formulated to seal the wall and help the finishing coats adhere properly. Priming is essential for a good finish coat, especially in a kitchen where frequent cleaning is necessary to remove cooking buildup.

Cutting in the primer on the ceiling.

Workday 11

Day 11 was when the homeowners began to see real progress and get a feel for how the kitchen would look. In the morning the painter applied the base coat to the primed walls and ceiling. After the paint dried, the decorative painting technique called sponging was applied to the walls.

In the morning the painter applied the base coat to the walls and ceilings in preparation for the faux finish.

"I like this technique (sponging) because you can be as dramatic as you want. You can bring in multiple colors and add some texture to the space. It also tends to hide imperfections. If you need to do any repairs, it doesn't have to be perfect."

—Gregg J. Kranzusch, Painter

"We selected this technique for a few reasons. There is a common wall in the dinette that runs into the living room. We needed a color that would work well in both rooms. We also wanted to have something that would complement the bold solid colors of the tile backsplash and the countertop."

—Lisa Egan, Homeowner

The decorative painter added patches of color to the base coat with a natural sea sponge.

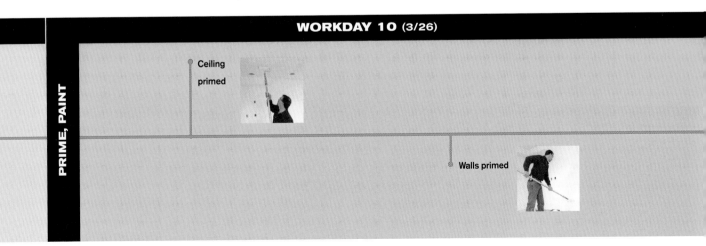

WORKDAY 10 (3/26)

PRIME, PAINT

Ceiling primed

Walls primed

Cabinet Installation
Workdays 12–14

Workday 12

Installation began on Day 12 of the project. The carpenter and an assistant worked with the new kitchen cabinets but faced a few problems. The house is old and nothing was exactly square, including the floors, the soffits, and the walls.

"You can't count on square and level in older houses, so you just have to take the time to level and shim until everything lines up. It's better to take the time now than to have things look off."

—*Rick Nadke, Contractor*

Because everything was slightly out of square, the installers took extra time to level as they hung the wall cabinets under the soffit.

Once all the wall units were in place, the installers immediately hung and adjusted the doors. Making these adjustments is easier before the base cabinets are installed.

At the end of the day, the wall cabinets are almost up and squared away.

WORKDAY 11 (3/28)

Base coat applied to walls and ceiling

Sponging technique applied to walls

Workday 13

It took a little longer than anticipated to hang the wall units, so installing the base cabinets didn't begin until Day 13. Because the base-cabinet layout was relatively simple, the installer worked with a single helper.

Since the homeowners didn't change the footprint of the old kitchen, the new cabinetry was similar in size and dimension to the old installation, which helped the installer anticipate problems he noticed when he removed the old cabinets.

Like the wall cabinets, the base cabinets took extra time because they required significant shimming to sit level on the out-of-square floor.

The corner base cabinet is installed first. The rest of the base cabinets follow on each side.

Base cabinets are leveled and attached to each other one by one, working down the line to the end of the run. The cabinets must be clamped securely together during assembly.

A cabinet installer will take great pains to ensure that each unit is square and level.

The plywood fascia is attached to the peninsula. Peninsulas require strong interior framing to maintain structural integrity.

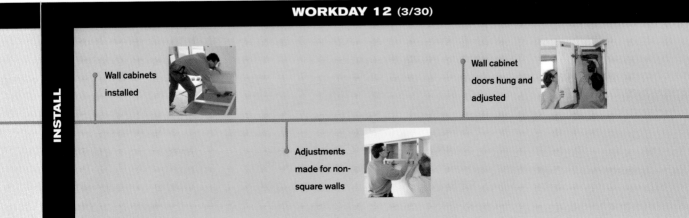

WORKDAY 12 (3/30)

INSTALL

Wall cabinets installed

Adjustments made for non-square walls

Wall cabinet doors hung and adjusted

Workday 14

Installing the base cabinets continued into Day 14. Contractor Rick Nadke continued to work on his own, but was making good time. His day would be spent finishing the base cabinetry, cutting a heating vent into one of the bases, and matching it to the duct for the vent already in the floor.

Rearranging elements in the kitchen exposed a new section of subflooring that had to be patched with the finished floor.

Having a smooth finished floor certainly makes cabinet installation easier, so flooring should be installed early in the process and protected during installation. With particularly expensive flooring, you may not want to waste material in areas that the cabinets will cover. If so, install the flooring after the cabinets are installed. Installing the flooring later in the process also protects it from damage during construction. Flooring should always be installed before the appliances are put into place.

Cutting the opening for the heating vent in the kickplate.

Measuring for the heating vent opening in the cabinet.

"The flooring installer we worked with earlier prefers to install the floors prior to the installation of any cabinetry. They said a smooth, level floor helps with cabinet installation. But it can be costly to install flooring that will not be seen."

—*John Egan, Homeowner*

Adding a side panel to connect the base and wall cabinets.

Using a circular saw to open up the area of the floor to be patched.

Using a chisel to clean up the area to be patched.

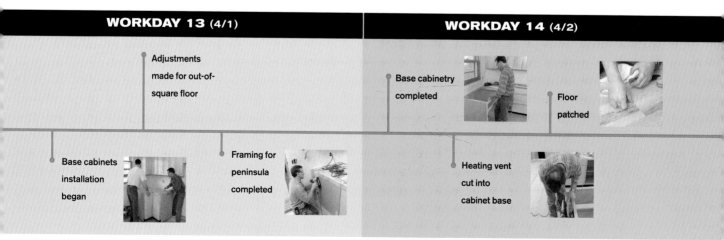

WORKDAY 13 (4/1)

Adjustments made for out-of-square floor

Base cabinets installation began

Framing for peninsula completed

WORKDAY 14 (4/2)

Base cabinetry completed

Floor patched

Heating vent cut into cabinet base

Countertop Installation

Workdays 15–16

Workday 15

The new kitchen is almost complete. With the cabinets in place, it was time for the countertops. The other big project of the day was installing the new range vent hood, which the contractor did before beginning on the countertops.

Initially the homeowners had explored solid-surfacing countertops, but they chose laminate to save money and invest the funds in more expensive cabinetry. The homeowners can upgrade the countertop in the future.

> *"We compromised on the counters so we could get some other things we wanted. It's always a trade-off—one thing for the other."*
> —Lisa Egan, Homeowner

Workday 16

Day 16 was spent finishing the countertops. The work needed to be completed because the electrician was scheduled to come in the next day to finish wiring the outlets and the fixtures. The sink area was prepared for installation. The tilers will set the backsplash in a few days.

Installing the range vent hood.

Test fitting the corner.

> *"Keeping things moving and on schedule is the hardest part of any remodel. You are dependent on the work going smoothly on-site as well as deliveries being made on schedule. Organization and good communication with the subcontractors and vendors are essential to keeping things on track."*
> —Rick Nadke, Contractor

Trimming the counter endcap.

Final fitting of the corner

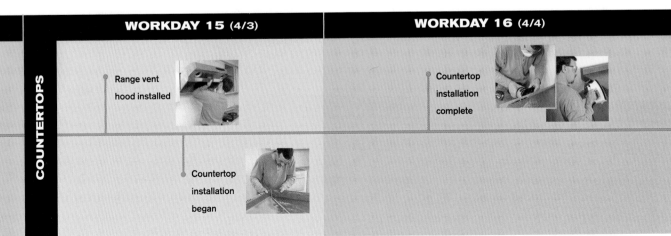

COUNTERTOPS

WORKDAY 15 (4/3)

Range vent hood installed

Countertop installation began

WORKDAY 16 (4/4)

Countertop installation complete

Finishing Up

Workdays 17–19

Workday 17

All remaining installation began on Day 17. The sink was cut into the countertop and hooked up to the drain and supply lines. The electrician's team wired the recessed lighting fixtures, installed countertop outlets, and hung the hanging fixture in the center of the dining area ceiling. After the sink was installed, the contractor put the knobs and hardware on the new cabinets.

Installing the sink.

Mounting the cabinet hardware.

"If you want to put a new sink into an old countertop, make sure it fits; you'd be surprised how often it doesn't. If the new sink is smaller, marks from the old one will show. Also if you're getting rid of the old sink and countertop, don't bother taking the sink out; just pull the whole unit."

—*Paul Keyes, Plumber*

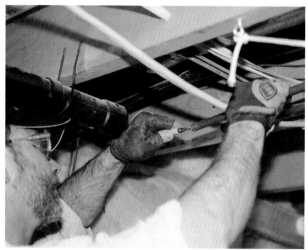
Running supply lines for the sink.

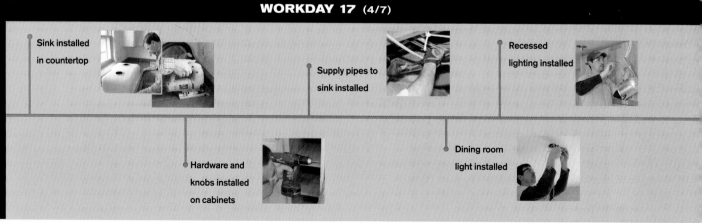

WORKDAY 17 (4/7)

Sink installed in countertop

Supply pipes to sink installed

Recessed lighting installed

Hardware and knobs installed on cabinets

Dining room light installed

PRIME, PAINT, INSTALL

Wiring the recessed fixtures.

Wiring countertop outlets.

Installing the recessed fixtures.

Workday 18

With installation almost finished, the tilers set the colorful backsplash. The Egans worked with the tilers to create the desired design. The homeowners did not want a distinct or checkerboard pattern. The tiles were placed randomly to avoid a formal diagonal pattern. While the tilers worked, the contractor installed kickplates on the base cabinets.

Installing kickplates.

Setting the tile backsplash.

WORKDAY 18 (4/8)

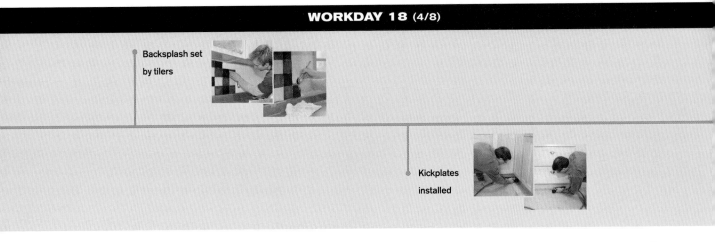

Backsplash set
by tilers

Kickplates
installed

Workday 19

While the contractor installed the appliances and completed the trim, the tiler grouted and cleaned the backsplash. After 19 on-site working days and five weeks of planning, the kitchen is finally finished.

Grouting the backsplash tile.

Installing the refrigerator.

BEFORE

AFTER

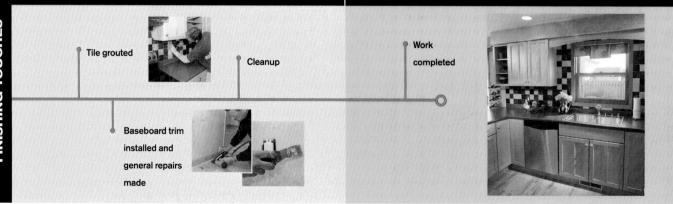

FINISHING TOUCHES

WORKDAY 19 (4/10)

Tile grouted

Cleanup

Baseboard trim installed and general repairs made

PROJECT FINISHED (4/11)

Work completed

Reality Check

"*The kitchen is the hub of our home. Having a pleasant, comfortable, and functional space makes it easy to use. From the kitchen you can access all levels of the house, so it truly is a central location.*

"*We like everything, but the new storage space on the old closet wall is great. We have plenty of functional storage and the recessed lighting gives us work areas that are well-lit. We enjoy the natural maple cabinets. The countertop, although not our first choice, was selected for color. We also wanted to incorporate color in the backsplash.*"

—*John and Lisa Egan, Homeowners*

The Egans' Final Numbers: $22,800

Fixtures and Appliances

■ **Cabinets:** The homeowners like the natural look of wood, and the floor was maple. It is a clean-looking wood with minimal graining and a simple door style. **Price: $8,000**

■ **Hardware:** John and Lisa wanted all stainless-steel hardware to coordinate with the sink and stainless-steel appliances. **Price: $350**

■ **Countertops:** This one was a compromise. The couple originally picked a solid-surfacing countertop, but after pricing it, they decided this surface was not so important. Solid-surfacing was almost as much as all the new cabinets. The laminate they chose was less than $1,000 and they selected the color and style to coordinate with the tile backsplash. **Price: $900**

■ **Sink:** The choice was stainless steel because the Egans felt it is easier to keep clean. **Price: $150**

■ **Faucet:** The couple liked the look of a faucet with a pullout spray feature. **Price: $150**

■ **Range hood:** They chose a stainless-steel ventilating hood. **Price: $200**

■ **Refrigerator:** The couple selected stainless-steel appliances because of the sleek look. It was important to have an icemaker feature and a wide side-by-side appliance. **Price: $1,900**

■ **Range:** They preferred an electric range over gas. Two ovens were considered necessary. The top oven can bake, toast, broil, and warm. The bottom can bake, broil, and convection bake. Both can be used at the same time. **Price: $1,700**

■ **Dishwasher:** The appliance had to be quiet and have a large capacity. **Price: $700**

Labor and Materials

■ Contractor/Remodeler:	$5,000
■ Plumber:	$300
■ Electrician	$1,100
■ Plasterer:	$950
■ Tile Setter:	$900
■ Painter:	$500

Contact Information and Resources

Contact Information

The Home Depot® offers kitchen products and materials from major manufacturers either in stock or through special order. This extensive inventory offers customers a comprehensive and varied selection that will ensure a kitchen that truly reflects their personal style, and taste while enabling them to stick to a realistic budget. Information on products and materials can be obtained from design centers in Home Depot stores or directly through manufacturers by mail, telephone, or online.

Contacting Meredith Corporation

To order this and other Meredith Corporation books call 800/678-8091. For further information about the information contained in this book, please contact the manufacturers listed or contact Meredith by e-mail at hi123@mdp.com or by phone at 800/678-2093.

Contacting The Home Depot

For general information about product availability contact your local Home Depot or visit The Home Depot® website at www.homedepot.com

Appliances
GE
GE Answer Center®
800/626-2000
www.geappliances.com

Jenn-Air
800/JennAir (800/536-6247)
www.jennair.com

Maytag Corporation
800/688-9900
www.maytag.com

Cabinetry and Hardware
American Woodmark
www.woodmark-homedepot.com
service@woodmark.com
540/665-9100

Amerock Corporation
800/435-6959

Berenson Hardware
www.berensonhardware.com

Häfele Cabinet Accessories
800/667-8721
www.haef.com

KraftMaid Cabinetry
800/571-1990
www.kraftmaid.com

Merillat Industries, LLC
800/575-8761
www.merillat.com

Mills Pride
Sold exclusively at The Home Depot®
www.millspride.com

Premier Cabinetry
www.premiercabinetry.com
customer_service@premiercabinetry.com
800/441-0337

Schrock Cabintery
www.schrock.com

Thomasville Cabinetry
www.thomasvillecabinetry.com
thomasville.cabinetry@homedepot.com
800/756-6497

Woodcrafters
800/235-7747 (Florida and Southwest division only)

Countertops & Backsplashes
Corian
800/4-CORIAN® (800/426-7426).
www.corian.com

Daltile
800-933-TILE
www.daltile.com

Pionite/Panolam
800/746-6483
www.pionite.com
Countertop–Chile Fiber, Suede (AO101-S)

Silestone by Cosentino
Cosentino USA
281/494-7277
www.silestoneusa.com

U.S. Ceramic Tile Company
www.usctco.com

Wilsonart
www.wilsonart.com

Flooring
Armstrong
www.armstrong.com

Bruce
800/236-2275
E-mail: totalat7359799@aol.com

Echeguren Slate, Inc.
800/992-0701
www.echeguren.com
Slate–Indian Silver Black

Pergo
800/33-PERGO (800/337-3746)
www.pergo.com

Total Floor Covering
800/236-2275
E-mail: totalat7359799@aol.com
Wilsonart
www.wilsonart.com

Lighting and Ceiling Fans
Georgia Lighting
www.georgialighting.com
866/544-4861

Hampton Bays
www.homedepot.com

Progress Lighting
www.homedepot.com

Plumbing and Fixtures
American Standard
800/524-9797 ext. 1007
www.americanstandard-us.com

Delta Faucet Company
www.deltafaucet.com

Eljer Plumbingware
E-mail: contactus@eljer.com
Phone: 877/355-3376
Fax: 877/460-2483

Elkay Sales, Inc.
www.elkayusa.com

Glacier Bay Faucets
Exclusively through The Home Depot®
www.glacierbayfaucets.com

GROHE America, Inc.
630/582-7711
www.groheamerica.com

International Thermocast
Sales Support e-mail:
    sales_support@thermocastsinks.com
Specific Sales Support:
    misti_deale@thermocastsinks.com
Phone: 678/445-2022
Fax: 678/445-2039
www.thermocastsinks.com

Insinkerator
800/558-5712
www.insinkerator.com

Kohler Co.
800/4-KOHLER (800/456-4537)
www.kohler.com

KWC Faucets Inc.
888/592-3287
www.kwcfaucets.com

Resources

Product Information

Listed below are the names and manufacturers of many of the products seen throughout the book. To find a product shown in a photograph, locate the product type (resources listed below) and the page number of the photo that interests you. Page numbers are next to manufacturers' names. To determine whether the product you are interested in, or its equivalent, is available to you, contact either your local Home Depot or the manufacturer. Contact information for each manufacturer is found on page 188. Most of the products, or their equivalent, are available through The Home Depot® either in stock or through special order, although there are some items shown that are unique to the locations where the photography was shot and may not be available. If the page number is not listed, no information about that particular product was available.

Colors

Please be aware that paint colors shown in the book may look different on your wall because of the printing process used in this book. If you see a color you like, show it to a Home Depot associate in the paint department, and he or she will custom-tint paint to match it as closely as possible. Buy samples of paint in small quantities and test areas so that you can see the result prior to spending time and money to paint an entire room. Changes in lighting affect colors, which, for instance, can seem remarkably different under artificial light and natural light. Also, for the sake of domestic harmony you may wish to consult everyone who will be living with the color. Paint a test area and live with it under different lighting conditions for at least 24 hours to make sure it is right for you.

Resource List

T=Top, C=Center, B=Bottom, L=Left, R=Right

Backsplash:

Total Floor Covering—5BR, 30B, 148CL, 168-169, 185CR, 186TL, 187

Cabinet Storage Accessories: ■

Häfele—133BC, 134TC, 134CC, 134CCR, 162CC, 163CL, 163CR, 163BR, 164BL, 165TL, 165TR, 165CR, 165BR ■ **KraftMaid**—133CL, 133BL, 134TL, 134TR, 134TCR, 134BL, 148-149

Cabinetry:

American Woodmark— 68, 70, 71, ■ **KraftMaid**—5TL, 8TR, 14CL, 15TR, 30B, 63, 64, 65, 66, 67, 87TL, 114CR, 122TR, 123TL, 123TR, 148-149, 168-169, 180-182, 184TR, 185, 186, 187 ■ **Merillat**—28B, 42-43, 44, 45, 46CL, 46BC, 47CL, 47BR ■ **Simon, Toney, & Fisher**—27BL ■ **Thomasville/Cologne**—72, 73-74

Cabinetry Hardware:

Amerock—14TR, 21T, 48-49, 50, 51TR, 51BL, 52BR, 53, 68, 70-71,131CR, 132TL, 132BL, 156–2nd row/C, 156–4th row/R ■ **Berenson Hardware**—28B, 42-43, 44, 45, 46CL, 46BC, ■ **KraftMaid**—05BR, 8TR, 30B, 63, 87TL, 114CR, 122TR, 123TL, 123TR, 148-149, 168-169, 184CL, 186, 187 ■ **Simon, Toney, & Fischer**—27BL ■ **Thomasville**—72, 73-74

Cooktops:

GE—63, 64, 72, 74, 92TL, 93TR, 143TR ■ **Jenn-Air**—18BL, 36CL, 38BR, 39B, 143CR

Countertops:

Corian—32TL, 63, 64, 65, 86CR, 100TL, 110TL, 113CL, 115TR, 115BR, 135TC, 148TL ■ **Daltile**—63 (backsplash) ■ **Pionite**—5BR, 30B, 68, 72, 135TL, 148CL, 168-169, 183, 187 ■ **Silestone**—6-7, 32-33, 136TR ■ **US Ceramic**—135TR

Dishwashers:

GE—44B, 45BL, 166CR, 166BC ■ **Jenn-Air**—21T, 48, 50BC, 51TR, 53BR, 92BR, 140CR, 140BL, 140BR ■ **Maytag**—5CR, 36BR, 39B, 68, 71TL, 72168, 186BR

Flooring:

Armstrong—68 ■ **Bruce**—63, 64, 65, 67 ■ **Echeguren Slate, Inc.**—32BL, 96TR, 147TL ■ **Pergo**—72

Freezers:

GE—139BL, 139BR

Island Bracket:

KraftMaid—152TR

Lighting:

Hampton Bay— 63, 64, 66, 67 ■ **Eurofase/Mya Pendant**—72, 74 ■ **Regal King/Track**—72

Microwaves:

GE—48, 50, TR, 63, 68, 70,145CR ■ **Jenn-Air**—84BR ■ **Maytag**—92BL, 145TR

Ovens (wall):

GE— 63, 72, 144C, 144BR,144BL ■ **Jenn-Air**—36BR, 39B, 144TR

Ranges:

GE—20TR, 28B, 31TR, 42-43, 44B, 45BR, 68, 70,110-111, 142TR, 142BL, 142BR, 160BL, 164CL, 166T ■ **Jenn-Air**—21T, 48-49, 50, 52BR, 83CR, 84BR, 142BR ■ **Maytag**—30B, 55, 57TL, 141TL, 142CL, 169, 187

Refrigerators:

GE—31TR, 44B, 45BL, 46CL, 47CL, 47BR, 63, 65, 68, 70, 72, 137TR, 137CR, 137BR, 160BL ■ **Jenn-Air**—50BC, 94BR, 110BL, 137TL ■ **Maytag**—30B, 186TR, 187BL

Refrigerator Features:

Jenn-Air—138TL, 138TR, 138TCL, 138TCR ■ **Maytag**—138BCL, 138BCR, 138BL, 138BR

Sink Accessories:

American Standard—112TL, 115TL

Sink Faucets:

American Standard—72, 95BL, 110CL, 112TL, 113TR, 115TL, 118TR, 118BR, 119TR, 119BL, 120CR ■ **Delta**—21T, 48, 50, 51TR, 51BL, 51BR, 68, 71TR, 113BR, 114BR, 121TL ■ **GROHE**—20BR ■ **Kohler**—28B, 30B, 44B, 45C, 63, 97TL, 115BL, 117BL, 117BC, 118BL, 120BR, 157BCL, 161TL, 162CR, 168, 184TR ■ **KWC**—18TR, 32CL, 157BCR

Sinks:

American Standard—95BL, 110CL, 112TL, 113TR, 115TL, 119TR, 119BL, 120CR ■ **Corian**—113CL, 115TR, 115BR ■ **Elkay**—18TR, 20BR, 30B, 72, 75, 97TL, 168, 184TR ■ **Kohler**—21T, 28B, 44B, 45C, 48, 50, 51TR, 51BL, 51BR, 63, 65, 68, 71TR, 113BR, 114BR, 115BL, 117BL, 117BC, 161TL, 162CR

Undercounter Refrigerators:

Magic Chef—139CR

Vent Hoods:

GE—31TR, 93TR, 160BL, 164CR, 166T

Washer/Dryer:

GE—67TR, 167TC

Wine Cooler:

GE—63, 139TC

Acknowledgments

Special Thanks to:
Tom and Lorena Ament
John and Lisa Egan
Paul and Jan Grant
Emily and Chris Kearns
Bonnie and David Krill
Lynn Mann-Hallmark and Don Hallmark
The Mantey Family
Doug Scheffler

National Kitchen & Bath Association
687 Willow Grove Street
Hackettstown, NJ 07840
877/NKBA-PRO (877/652-2776)
www.nkba.com

The Center for Universal Design
North Carolina State University
Campus Box 8613
Raleigh, NC 27695-8613
www.design.ncsu.edu/cud

Chapter 2

Pages 34–41
Decorative Painting: Don Soderberg Painting
Mike Rowlings, Milwaukee, Wisconsin
414/771-1288
Furnishings: Peabody's Interiors
Lisa Minneti, Whitefish Bay, Wisconsin
414/962-4550
Interior Decorator: Emily Kearns
Mequon, Wisconsin

Pages 42–47
Decorator: Lynn Mann-Hallmark
Milwaukee, Wisconsin

Pages 48–53
Flooring and Countertops: Total Floor
Covering, Appleton, Wisconsin
800/236-2275
E-mail: totalat7359799@aol.com
Interior Design Consultant: Cynthia Mantey
Green Bay, Wisconsin
920/884-3182

Pages 54–61
Designer/Decorator: Bonnie Krill
Cedar Grove, Wisconsin

Pages 62–67
Architect: Jeff Hibbard Design Services, Inc.
(920) 731-7365
hibbarddesign@aol.com
Builder: Tom Ament
Kaukauna, Wisconsin
(920) 766-7900
tja@wiscobuilds.com
Interior Design: Elite Home Creations
Deb Van Straten
(920) 419-1789
elitehomes@new.rr.com

Interior Decorating: Kathy Mitchell
Menasha, Wisconsin
(920) 729-6006
redesigns@ameritech.net

Page 68
Power Access Automatic Door Opener
by Power Access Corporation
170 Main Street
New Hartford, CT
06057
1-800-344-0088

Chapter 6

Pages 158–167
Architect/Project Manager: Rosemann &
Associates, Eddie Tapper
Kansas City, Missouri
816/472-1448
www.rosemann.com

Property Owner/Executive Director:
Universal Design Housing Network
Paul Levy
Kansas City, MO
816/751-7898
www.udhn.org

Interior Design: American Society of Interior
Designers, Missouri-West/Kansas Chapter
Carolyn Wear, ASID
913/268-9126
Doreen Gregory, ASID
913/341-5917
Sallie Kytt Redd, ASID
913/492-3158
Sheryl Koch, ASID
816/537-0133
Kelly Stewart
816/803-0036
Deborah Cook
816/313-8104
Suzette Burton
888/471-1715

Chapter 7

Pages 168–187
Kitchen and Bath Design Center:
Beth Loerke, Home Depot #4903
Electrical: Team Services
Appleton, Wisconsin
920/738-5885
E-mail: julief@new.rr.com
Tile Backsplash: Total Floor Covering,
Appleton, Wisconsin
800/236-2275
E-mail: totalat7359799@aol.com
Painting: Gregg J. Kranzusch Painting
Neenah, Wisconsin
Plastering: Uitenbroek Plastering Inc.
Appleton, Wisconsin
920/749-0787

Plumbing: Keyes & Sons Plumbing
& Heating, Inc.
Appleton, Wisconsin
920/725-2494

Want to do it yourself?

If you're interested in renovating or remodeling your kitchen on your own The Home Depot® 1-2-3 library offers clear and concise step-by-step, project-driven books to help you through the process.

Titles include: *Home Improvement 1-2-3*, *Decorating 1-2-3*, *Decorative Painting 1-2-3*, *Wiring 1-2-3*, *Plumbing 1-2-3*, *Flooring 1-2-3*, and *Tiling 1-2-3*. These books are available at The Home Depot and at bookstores throughout North America.

Index

Toolbox essentials: nuts-and-bolts books for do-it-yourself success.

Save money, get great results, and take the guesswork out of home improvement projects with a growing library of step-by-step books from the experts at The Home Depot®.

Packed with lots of projects and practical tips, these books help you design, remodel, decorate, and repair your home or garden. Easy-to-follow, step-by-step instructions and colorful photographs ensure success. Projects even estimate time, skills, materials needed, and tools required.

Look for the books that help you say "I can do that!" at The Home Depot,® www.meredithbooks.com, or wherever quality books are sold.